D!RTY®
RUSSIAN

Everyday Slang from "What's Up?" to "F*%# Off!"

SECOND EDITION

ERIN COYNE AND IGOR FISUN

illustrated by LINDSAY MACK

ULYSSES PRESS

*To Myroslava. Someday this book
is gonna embarrass the hell out of you.*

Published by:
Ulysses Press
PO Box 3440
Berkeley, CA 94703
www.ulyssespress.com

ISBN: 978-1-64604-258-6
Library of Congress Control Number: 2021937738

Printed in the United States by Kingery Printing Company
20 19 18 17 16 15 14 13 12 11 10 9

Managing editor: Claire Chun
Project manager: Kierra Sondereker
Interior design: what!design @ whatweb.com
Cover design: Double R Design
Back cover illustration: Lindsay Mack
Interior art: Lindsay Mack except cocktail glass © Svitlana
    Medvedieva/shutterstock.com
Cocktail recipes: Katy Chapman and Chrissy McIntyre,
    The Barlingual Chicks

TABLE OF CONTENTS

USING THIS BOOK

Russian is just about the coolest language in the world. But you already know that because you've been studying the language for a while now, right? At least I hope you have, because I didn't write this book with the novice in mind. I designed the book to bring your Russian to the next level, a level usually reserved for natives and longtime expats. With that in mind, I've tried to give you all the dirty words and insider terms that your college Russian professor would never teach you. So you're not gonna find any basic vocabulary or grammar lessons, or ways to ask somebody where the library is. It's assumed that you know all that crap already. But if you're looking to tell somebody to fuck off or that they've got a nice ass, then you're in the right place, my friend.

All of this is to say that I hope you already more or less know your way around the language before jumping into this book. It is a complex language to master even at a fairly basic level. Learning the slang is even harder as it can be extremely difficult for the uninitiated to gauge when, where, and with whom slang is appropriate. As the old saying goes: when in doubt, leave it out. Using the wrong slang with the wrong person at the wrong time—especially with a strong foreign accent—will make you sound ridiculous. It really will. So err on the side of caution. Also be aware that it is far less socially acceptable for women to use foul language, so know your audience before letting it rip.

That being said, I did try to make the book as reader friendly as possible. Each phrase in the book is accompanied by its English equivalent and its Russian pronunciation. Often you'll find example sentences with key slang words bolded so you can break those words out and employ them on your own, whether you're just joking around with your friends at school or spending quality time on the streets of Moscow, St. Petersburg, Kiev, or some remote backwater village. Once you start to know your way around and find yourself with a group of sailor-mouthed friends with three days' worth of drinkin' on their breath, you should jump right in and start throwing the slang around. Even clumsy attempts will likely earn their amused affection.

Now take your *Dirty Russian* and get dirty with it.

·····Some Basics

Russian, much like Russia itself, is not for the faint of heart. So here are a few notes to keep in mind as you're reading:

Ty and Vy: Like many languages, Russian has two pronouns for "you": *ty* and *vy*. *Ty* is the informal and singular way of saying "you"; *vy* is formal and plural. We have used *ty* as the default in this book as slang is something inherently linked to informal social situations. Generally, you wouldn't say anything in this book to someone that you are on *vy* with. *Vy*, however, is also used for plurals, so this is the one you need when talking to more than one person.

Cases: Russian has six grammatical cases, which means that the endings of words change depending on their function in the sentence (direct object, indirect object, object of a preposition, etc.). When words are given in isolation, assume that they are in the nominative case. However, when they are given in phrases, they have whatever case ending is necessary for the grammatical context. As this is not a first-year Russian textbook, familiarity of basic Russian grammar is presumed. If none of this paragraph made sense to you, go look it up.

Gender: All Russian nouns have a gender (masculine, feminine, or neuter). This is important because it will affect the declensional patterns as well as the endings you use on the adjectives to describe nouns. In terms of people, gender means that both adjectives and the past tense of verbs take different endings depending on whether you are talking about a man or a woman. In most cases, we have used masculine endings as a sort of "default" gender. Feminine endings are used only when specified as such. If that seems sexist to anyone, well, what can I say? That's Russia—you might as well get used to it now.

Pronunciation: The most important thing when it comes to pronunciation in Russian is stress. Once you find the correct stressed syllable in a word, the rest of the pronunciation should fall into place. In this book, stress is indicated in the transliteration line by capital letters. There are some finer points of pronunciation that aren't as essential, such as voicing and devoicing. If you screw those up, you'll sound totally foreign, but you'll still be understood.

·····Slang
slyeng
Сленг

Here are some relevant terms before we begin:

Jargon
zhar-GON
Жаргон
Another term that basically means "slang," but most often used when talking about criminal slang.

Cussing
ru-GA-tyel-stvo
Ругательство

Obscene language
mat
Мат

To curse using obscene language
ma-tye-RIT-sya
Матерится

To cuss
ru-GAT-sya MA-tom
Ругаться матом

Curse words
MA-tyer-ni-ye slo-VA
Матерные слова

Indecent language
nye-nor-ma-TIV-na-ya LYEK-si-ka
Ненормативная лексика
This is a phrase you'll see, for example, on the warning label on CDs, etc.

·····Pronouncing Russian

Here's the Russian alphabet. Most of it isn't too tricky, but there are few sounds that differ from English.

Аа sounds like "ah," as in "open your mouth and say 'ah.'"

Бб sounds like "b." At the end of a word, it sounds like "p."

Вв sounds like "v." At the end of a word, it sounds like "f."

Гг sounds like g. At the end of a word, it is pronounced "k."

Ее sounds like "yeh." If unstressed, it usually sounds more like "ee."

Ёё sounds like "yo," as in "Yo!" This letter can only appear in stressed positions, so if a word changes stress when put into a different case, this letter falls out and becomes a regular ol' **e**.

Жж sounds like "zh," like the *g* in "massage." This consonant is always hard; at the end of a word, it sounds like "sh."

Зз sounds like "z." At the end of a word, it is pronounced "s."

Ии sounds like "ee," as in "Eeek!"

Йй sounds like "y," sort of like the *y* in "day."

Кк sounds like "k."

Лл sounds like "l."

Мм sounds like "m."

Нн sounds like "n."

Оо sounds like "o," as in "folk." If unstressed, it is pronounced like an "a."

Пп sounds like "p."

Рр sounds like "r." This is trilled.

Сс sounds like "s."

Тт sounds like "t."

Уу sounds like "oo," as in "boot."

Фф sounds like "f."

Хх sounds like "kh," sort of like the *ch* in "achtung."

Цц sounds like "ts." This consonant is always hard.

Чч sounds like "ch." This consonant is always soft.

Шш sounds like "sh." This consonant is always hard.

Щщ sounds like "sch," like "fresh chicken." This consonant is always soft.

ъ is a hard sign. This causes the preceding consonant to harden.

ы sounds like saying "it" and "eat" at the same time. If you can do that, then you'll be pretty close. If you can't do that, err on the side of *i* in "it."

ь is a soft sign. This softens the preceding consonant.

Ээ sounds like "eh."

Юю sounds like "yu."

Яя sounds like "ya." If unstressed, it usually sounds closer to "ee."

Some combined sounds:

ай sounds like "ay," as in "ay, carumba!"

ой sounds like "oy," as in "boy." If unstressed, it's "ay."

ей sounds like "ei," as in "weight."

дж sounds like "j," as in "Joe."

CHAPTER 1

HOWDY RUSSIAN

PRI-VYET-LIVII RU-SSKII
Приветливый русский

Greetings in Russia are pretty much like everywhere else; there's some version of "Hello," "How are you?", etc. No real trick, except that you need to remember who you're talking to. If you're talking to someone you don't know very well who's over the age of, say, 30, stick with the formal *Vy*. With younger people, you can pretty safely use the informal *ty*, especially if you are in a chill social situation among friends. Keep in mind that using *ty* with the wrong person in Russia is a pretty serious insult that will piss some people off.

·····Howdy!
ZDRA-sstye!
Здрассте!

Saying hello seems simple enough, right? Well, it is. But if you're guy and don't shake on it, you'll be considered a total asshole. If you're a chick and do the same, they'll think you're, well, foreign and a little weird. And if you're greeting someone you know fairly well, there'll be kissing involved, whether you like it or not. Russians in general have a much

🍸 MOSCOW MULE

Okay, so the Moscow Mule was not invented in Russia. So what? It's the perfect cocktail to start your Russian adventure with the country's signature spirit, vodka.

GET THESE:
2 ounces vodka
4 ounces ginger beer (or more, to taste)
1 ounce freshly squeezed lime juice
lime slice, for garnish

DO THIS:
Combine the vodka, ginger beer, and fresh lime juice in a tall glass or copper Moscow Mule cup, if you have one. Fill to the rim with ice and stir until combined and well chilled. Garnish with a slice of lime. Down it quickly and make another, because you're in Russia now, baby.

different concept of personal space than Americans, so just suck it up, say your hellos, and move on.

Hi!
pri-VYET!
Привет!

Hiya!
pri-VYET-iki!
Приветики!
Kinda cutesy.

Sup guys!
zdo-RO-vo, re-BYA-ta!
Здорово, ребята!
Remember to watch your stress with this word. The greeting is *zdo-RO-vo*. With the stress *ZDO-ro-vo*, it means something more like "awesome."

Hey, buddy!
pri-VYET, dru-ZHI-sche!
Привет, дружище!

Shout out to all the cool peeps in the house!
khai vsyem nor-MAL-nim PI-plam!
Хай всем нормальным пиплам!

What's up?
kak de-LA?
Как дела?

How ya doin'?
kak ti?
Как ты?

What's new?
chto NO-vo-vo?
Что нового?

How's life?
kak zhi-VYOSH?
Как живёшь?

What's the word?
chto SLISH-no?
Что слышно?

What's cookin'?
kak zhizn mo-lo-DA-ya?
Как жизнь молодая?

Hey, honey, wassuuup?
*pri-VYET, kra-SOT-ka, kak **del-ISH-ki**?*
Привет, красотка, как **делишки**?
Kinda cutesy.

•••••Everything's just hunky-dory
vsyo i-DYOT kak po MA-slu
Всё идёт как по маслу

When I talk to Russians who have been to the U.S., the one thing that they all say annoys the crap out of them is the insincerity of the American "How are you?" greeting. It's because that question is always answered with a big, stupid grin and an "I'm fine" no matter how obvious it is that the person is in a shitty, pissed-off mood. It doesn't matter if the person just got herpes from their sister, they'll still answer "I'm fine." So when Russians ask you how you are, go ahead and tell them the truth. They asked for it.

It's all good!
vsyo kho-ro-SHO!
Всё хорошо!

Everything's A-OK.
vsyo o-KEI.
Всё о-кей.

Fine.
nor-MAL-no.
Нормально.

Fine 'n' dandy.
CHI-ki PI-ki.
Чики-пики.

Peachy.
CHU-denko.
Чудненько.

Super duper!
SU-per PU-per!
Супер пупер!

Couldn't be better!
LU-chshe vsyekh!
Лучше всех!

Pretty fuckin' good!
pi-ZDA-to!
Пиздато!

Fucking awesome!
za-ye-BIS!
Заебись!
The word can either mean "really good" or "really fucking awful," depending on how you use it.

Everything's all right.
u me-NYA vsyo v po-RYAD-kye.
У меня всё в порядке.

I'm fresh as a daisy.
ya SVYE-zhii kak o-GUR-chik.
Я свежий как огурчик.
Literally, "fresh as a cucumber." This is usually said by someone in denial about how shitfaced they are.

No worries.
vsyo po ti-KHON-ku.
Всё по тихоньку.

Same old, same old.
vsyo po STA-romu.
Всё по старому.

What's it to ya?
kak-O-ye te-BYE DYE-lo?
Какое тебе дело?

What do you care?
kak-A-ya te-BYE RA-zni-tsa?
Какая тебе разница?

Don't even ask!
nye SPRA-shi-vai!
Не спрашивай!

Lousy as hell!
POL-nii ab-ZATS!
Полный абзац!

Pretty crappy.
khren-O-vo.
Хреново.

Really shitty.
khu-yO-vo.
Хуёво.

I'm in a crappy mood.
ya v kher-O-vom na-stro-yE-ni-ye.
Я в херовом настроении.

I must have gotten up on the wrong side of the bed today.
ya na-VYER-no se-VOD-nya vstal s LYE-voi no-GI.
Я наверное сегодня встал с левой ноги.

My life has turned into a total nightmare.
*mo-YA zhizn pre-vra-TI-las v **splosh-NOI kosh-MAR**.*
Моя жизнь превратилась **в сплошной кошмар**.

Really sucky.
POL-na-ya ZHO-pa.
Полная жопа.
Literally, "total ass."

Fucking awful!
ya v piz-DYE!
Я в пизде!
Literally, "I'm in the pussy."

Totally fucked up!
POL-nii piz-DYETS!
Полный пиздец!
If you want to soften this phrase up a bit, you can use the word
пипец (*pi-PYETZ*), which is a sort of euphemistic form of the
word пиздец.

That's the dealio.
vot ta-KI-ye pi-rozh-KI.
Вот такие пирожки.
Usually said after a detailed explanation of what has happened
to you recently.

·····Hell if I know
chort ye-VO ZNA-yet
Чёрт его знает

There are only 24 hours in a day, so there's just no way that
you can be expected to know everything about everything
that's going on around you.

I don't know.
ya nye ZNA-yu.
Я не знаю.

I'm out of the loop.
ya nye v KUR-sye.
Я не в курсе.

This is the first I've heard of it.
PYER-vii raz SLI-shu.
Первый раз слышу.

I have no idea.
po-NYA-ti-ya ne I-me-yu.
Понятия не имею.

Time will tell.
po-zhi-VYOM, u-VI-dim.
Поживём, увидим.

What's that thingamajig?
*chto E-to za **khren-o-TYEN**?*
Что это за **хренотень**?

God only knows.
bog ye-VO ZNA-yet.
Бог его знает.

Damned if I know.
khryen ye-VO ZNA-yet.
Хрен его знает.

Fuck if I know.
khui ye-VO ZNA-yet.
Хуй его знает.

How would I know?
ot-KU-da ya ZNA-yu?
Откуда я знаю?

How should I know?
ot-KU-da mnye znat?
Откуда мне знать?

There's just no understanding Russia.
u-mOm ro-SSI-yu nye po-NYAT.
Умом Россию не понять.

You can usually score some cultural points with this famous line from a poem by Fyodor Tyutchev.

·····Let's be friends!
BU-dyem dru-ZYA-mi!
Будем друзьями!

In America, we tend to be polite to strangers but then turn around and treat our friends like shit because, hey, they'll forgive us. Russians are sort of the opposite: They tend to be total assholes to strangers but fiercely loyal and embarrassingly generous to those they consider part of their inner circle. So here are a few phrases to help you break the ice with your new Russian acquaintances and maybe make yourself an ally in the process.

Let's use *ty*.
da-VAI na ti.
Давай на ты.
Once you start getting to know someone better, this is the way that you suggest taking the next step and moving to the informal "you."

Could you show me around the city?
ti bi nye mog mnye GO-rod po-ka-ZAT?
Ты бы не мог мне город показать?

You wanna come over to my place?
KHO-chesh ko mnye v GO-sti?
Хочешь ко мне в гости?

Let's shoot the breeze!
da-VAI po-bol-TA-yem!
Давай поболтаем!

Let's hang out a bit.
da-VAI po-ob-SCHA-yem-sya.
Давай пообщаемся.

I feel like **shooting the shit** with someone.
*KHO-chet-sya s kyem-to **po-piz-DYET**.*
Хочется с кем-то **попиздеть**.

I don't know anyone here, but I'd like to **meet some cool guys.**
*ya ni-ko-VO ne ZNA-yu tut, no kho-TYEL-os bi **po-zna-KO-mit-sya s KLA-ssni-mi re-BYA-ta-mi***.
Я никого не знаю тут, но хотелось бы **познакомиться с классными ребятами**.

I hope I'll find some **common ground** with them.
*na-DYE-yus, nai-DU s NI-mi **O-bschii ya-ZIK***.
Надеюсь, найду с ними **общий язык**.

•••••Long time no see!
SKOI-ko lyet SKOI-ko zim!
Сколько лет сколько зим!

I don't get around as much as I used to, so when I do hit the town, it is always nice to run into an old pal. When a familiar face appears, go ahead and tell them how nice it is to see them.

Who do I see there!
ko-VO ya VI-zhu!
Кого я вижу!

Where ya been keepin' yourself?
ku-DA ti pro-PAL?
Куда ты пропал?

What are you guys doing here!
kak-I-ye LYU-di!
Какие люди!

Speak of the devil!
LYO-gok na po-MI-nye!
Лёгок на помине!

Hey, old man, good to see you!
*eh, sta-rRIK, **rad te-BYA VI-dyet**!*
Эй, старик, **рад тебя видеть**!

I've missed you!
ya po te-BYE so-SKU-chil-sya!
Я по тебе соскучился!

·····Please and thank you
po-ZHA-lui-sta i spa-SI-bo
Пожалуйста и спасибо

If you've studied any Russian at all, then you know that one of the funny things about the language is that "please" and "you're welcome" are the same word: пожалуйста. This can start to sound a little lame after a while: пожалуйста, спасибо, пожалуйста, спасибо, on and on and on and on. So if you want to avoid sounding like a broken record, here a few phrases you can use to add a little variety into the mix.

I have a request for you.
u me-NYA k te-BYE PRO-sba.
У меня к тебе **просьба**.

Be a pal!
bud DRU-gom!
Будь другом!

Help me out!
bud lyu-BYE-zen!
Будь любезен!

I'm really asking you!
ya te-BYA O-chen prosh-U!
Я тебя очень прошу!

I'm begging you!
ya te-BYA u-mo-LYA-yu!
Я тебя умоляю!

I'm very grateful.
ya O-chen bla-go-DA-ren.
Я очень благодарен.
This is pretty formal and official sounding.

I thank you.
bla-go-dar-IU.
Благодарю.
This is also kind of formal but is sometimes used ironically by young people.

Thanky!
spa-SI-boch-ki!
Спасибочки!
Kind of a cutesy way of saying thanks.

SURPRISE)))
U-DI-VLE-NI-YE
УДИВЛЕНИЕ

Life in Russia is full of surprises. Which might be why they have so many words and expressions that essentially all mean "wow."

Wow!	*vau!*	Вау!
Wowzers!	*ukh, ti!*	Ух, ты!
Word.	*ye-SCHO bi.*	Ещё бы.
Well, how'd ya like that!	*nu, ti da-YOSH!*	Ну, ты даёшь!
Well, dang!	*o-bal-DYET!*	Обалдеть!
That's wild!	*o-fi-GYET!*	Офигеть!
I'll be damned!	*o-du-RYET!*	Одуреть!
Fuckin' A!	*o-khu-YET!*	Охуеть!
Holy shit!	*khu-YA-sye!*	Хуясе!
Holy fuck!	*za-ye-BIS!*	Заебись!
That's fucked up!	*Ɛ-ta piz-DYETZ!*	Это пиздец!
Fuck!	*yob!*	Ёб!
Not bad!	*ni-che-VO se-BYƐ!*	Ничего себе!
Holy cow!	*ni fig-A se-BYƐ!*	Ни фига себе!
Hot damn!	*ni khren-A se-BYƐ!*	Ни хрена себе!
Fuck yeah!	*ni khu-YA se-BYƐ!*	Ни хуя себе!

These last four are also often used sarcastically; for example, when you think someone has acted really out of line and you say to yourself, "You gotta be kiddin' me."

·····No problem!
byez pro-BLYEM!
Без проблем!

If you're friends with a Russian, it's pretty much taken for granted that you'll be willing to lend a hand when needed without complaint and generally without too many questions. Here a few ways to tell your Russian pal that you're cool with that.

Don't mention it.
NYE za chto
Не за что.
Here is another place where you need to be careful with stress. To say "Don't mention it," you have to stress it *NYE za chto*. If you say *nye za CHTO*, it means something like "No way, no how."

Don't worry about it!
da LAD-no!
Да ладно!

It's not worth (mentioning)!
nye STO-it!
Не стоит!
Yet another place where stress is important. Here you need *nye STO-it*. If you say *nye sto-IT*, you'll be saying "It doesn't stand."

Easy-peasy!
ZA-pro-sto!
Запросто!

No biggie!
da E-to fig-NYA!
Да это фигня!

Nothin' to it!
NYE fig DYE-lat!
Не фиг делать!

Enjoy it (in health)!
na zdo-RO-vye!
На здоровье!

GETTiNG TO KNOW YOU)))

ZNAKOMSTVO
ЗНАКОМСТВО

I'm John.
ya—dzhon.
Я—Джон.

I think I'm pretty cool, but my friends all say I'm a loser.
ya schi-TA-yu se-BYA kru-TIM, no vsye mo-I dru-ZYA go-vo-RYAT, chto ya LU-zer.
Я считаю себя крутым, но все мои друзья
говорят, что я лузер.

I'm really **just misunderstood and very lonely**.
na SA-mom DYEL-ye, me-NYA nye po-ni-MA-yut i ya O-chen o-di-NOK.
На самом деле, меня не понимают и я очень
одинок.

Will you be my friend?
BU-dye-te mo-IM DRU-gom?
Будете моим другом?

The honeys ain't bad here.
DYE-vki tut ni-che-VO.
Девки тут ничего.

I have a huge penis.
u men-YA o-GRO-mnii chlyen.
У меня огромный член.

My name is Mary.
Men-YA zo-VUT ME-ri.
Меня зовут Мэри.

I've come to Russia **in search of love**.
ya pri-YE-kha-la v ro-SSI-yu v POI-skakh lyu-BVI.
Я приехала в Россию в поисках любви.

I like candlelit dinners, long walks on the beach, and wild sex.
mnye NRA-vit-sya U-zhi-nat pri SVYE-chkakh, DOl-gi-ye pro-GUL-ki na PLYA-zhe, i bez-U-mnii seks.
Мне нравится ужинать при свечах, долгие
прогулки на пляже, и безумный секс.

My vagina is cavernous.
Mo-YA va-GI-na kak pe-SCHE-ra.
Моя вагина как пещера.

·····My bad!

iz-vi-NYA-yus!
Извиняюсь!

Sooner or later you're going to make an ass of yourself.
You just are. So here are few ways to say a quick apology
and shake it off.

Excuse me!
iz-vi-NI!
Извини!

Forgive me!
pro-STI!
Прости!

Sorry!
SO-ri!
Сори!
Just like English, only with a Russian *o* and a rolled *r*.

Whoops!
O-pa!
Опа!

Oops!
ups!
Упс!

For God's sake, forgive me!
pro-STI me-NYA, RA-di BO-ga!
Прости меня, ради Бога!

Believe it or not, I really didn't mean to offend you.
vyer nye VYER, ya nye kho-TYEL te-BYA o-BI-dyet.
Верь не верь, я не хотел тебя обидеть.

I was just kidding.
ya po-shu-TIL.
Я пошутил.

I don't know what's wrong with me.
ya nye ZNA-yu, chto so mnoi.
Я не знаю, что со мной.

I'm such an idiot.
ya tak-OI i-di-OT.
Я такой идиот.

It's all my fault.
ya vo vsyom vi-no-VAT.
Я во всём виноват.

Don't be upset with me!
nye o-bi-ZHAI-sya!
Не обижайся!

I frickin' swear I didn't do it on purpose!
BLYA BU-du, ya nye spye-tsi-AL-no!
Бля буду, я не специально!

·····Let's roll!
AI-da!
Айда!

Russians aren't known for being in a hurry, and parties, casual meetings, and even chance encounters can quickly become long, drawn out, and downright tiresome. Here a few verbal cues to let your friends know that you're ready to make a getaway.

Bye!
ko-KA!
Пока!

See ya later!
do VSTRYE-chi!
До встречи!

See ya soon!
do SKO-ro-vo!
До скорого!

Kiss, kiss!
tsium, tsium!
Цюм, цюм!

Don't be a stranger!
ne pro-pa-DAI!
Не пропадай!

Ciao!
chau!
Чау!

It's time for us (to go)!
nam po-RA!
Нам пора!

I'm off!
ya po-SHOL!
Я пошёл!

Let's fucking bail already!
po-PIZ-di-li u-ZHE!
Попиздили уже!

It's time for me to get the fuck outta here.
mnye po-RA sye-BAT-sya.
Мне пора съебаться.

It's getting kinda late.
u-ZHE ne-DYET-sko-ye VRYE-mya.
Уже недетское время.

I'll call you.
ya te-BYE po-zvo-NIU.
Я тебе позвоню.

▪▪▪▪▪Hey, you!
eh, ti!
Эй, ты!

Sometimes you just want to give a shout out to someone you see on the street. Here are some quick ways to get their attention.

Hey...!
eh...!
Эй...!

little girl
DYE-voch-ka
девочка
This is generally used for a girl up to about age 12 or so.

young man
mo-lo-DOI che-lo-VYEk
молодой человек
This can be used for any guy up to about age 30.

miss
DYE-vu-shka
девушка
This is for females up to about age 30.

ma'am
ZHEN-schi-na
женщина
For women over 30 or so.

lady
BA-rish-nya
барышня

grandma
BA-bu-shka
бабушка
For old ladies; just try to resist the American urge to say *ba-BU-shka*. It's *BA-bu-shka*, dammit.

granny
ba-BU-lya
бабуля
Also for old ladies, but probably somewhat more common in small towns and villages.

gramps
dye-DU-lya
дедуля

old man
sta-RIK
старик

pal
pri-YA-tyel
приятель

buddy
dru-ZHOK
дружок

comrade
to-VA-risch
товарищ
Mainly used by old communists and ironic young people.

citizen
gra-zhda-NIN
гражданин
This is pretty Soviet sounding but still occasionally used.

guys
re-BYA-ta
ребята

homey
pa-TSAN
пацан

bro
bra-TAN
братан

dude
chu-VAK
чувак

Russian doesn't make very wide use of titles. When Russians want to address someone formally, they use the name and patronymic formula (you know, like Иван Иванович) instead of Mister, Ms., etc. When titles are used, it is mainly with foreigners who expect that sort of thing. Also, most foreign names don't lend themselves well to Russification and end up sounding pretty silly when you try. So for those occasions:

Mister
go-spo-DIN
Господин

Ms.
go-spo-ZHA
Госпожа

In formal public speeches, you may also sometimes hear:

Ladies and gentlemen!
DA-mi i go-spo-DA!
Дамы и господа!

CHAPTER 2

FRIENDLY RUSSIAN

DRU-ZHE-SKII RU-SSKII
Дружеский русский

In the U.S., we tend to call just about everyone we know our "friends." Russians are not nearly so casual about relationships, however. To them a friend is someone who has been through thick and thin with you, someone who would share his last beer with you and bail you out of jail. For all those other people that you just hang out with, there are different words to describe the more casual nature of your relationship.

·····Friends
dru-ZYA
Друзья

You're a good friend (male/female)
ti kho-RO-shii drug/kho-RO-sha-ya po-DRU-ga.
Ты **хороший друг/хорошая подруга.**

He is my very **best friend** in the world.
*on moi SA-mii **LU-chshii drug** v MI-rye.*
Он мой самый **лучший друг** в мире.

🍸 TOLSTOY COCKTAIL

Invented by the Russian Standard Original Vodka company to celebrate the 18th anniversary of Russia's independence, you'll want to drink this cocktail to the last drop, and then order another.

GET THESE:
2 ounces Russian Standard Vodka
1 ounce freshly squeezed lemon juice
¼ ounce simple syrup*

DO THIS:
Combine all of the ingredients in a cocktail shaker filled with ice. Shake vigorously for 20 to 30 seconds, until very cold. Strain into a martini glass for a "straight up" cocktail, or into a rocks glass filled with ice for "on the rocks" style. Either way, you can't go wrong.

* For simple syrup: Add equal parts sugar and water to a saucepan. Heat gently until the sugar is dissolved. Pour into a clean glass jar and store in your refrigerator for up to 1 month.

Me and my **buddies** usually go shoot the shit after work.
*mi so svo-I-mi **pri-YA-tel-ya-mi** o-BI-chno KHO-dim po-pi-ZDYET PO-sle ra-BO-ti.*
Мы со своими **приятелями** обычно ходим попиздеть после работы.
This is a friend of a more casual nature, someone you just shoot the shit with.

Hey, **homies**, let's party!
*eh, **pa-tsa-NI**, da-VAi po-tu-SU-yem-sya!*
Эй, **пацаны**, давай потусуемся!

Dudes, let's go for a beer.
***mu-zhi-KI**, poi-DYOM za PI-vom.*
Мужики, пойдём за пивом.

My (high school) **classmate** always uses a cheat sheet.
*moi **od-no-KLA-ssnik** vsye-GDA i-SPOL-zu-yet shpar-GAL-ku.*
Мой **одноклассник** всегда использует шпаргалку.

He's my (college) classmate at the uni.
*on moi **od-no-KURS-nik** v u-ni-VER-ye.*
Он мой **однокурсник** в универе.

We're roommates in the dorm.
*mi **so-SYE-di po KO-mna-tye** v ob-SCHA-gye.*
Мы **соседи по комнате** в общаге.

I saw my boyfriend last night with some ho.
*ya vch-RA VI-dye-la svo-ye-VO **boi-FREND-a** s ka-KOI-to BLA-dyu.*
Я вчера видела своего **бойфренда** с какой-то блядью.

My girlfriend is coming over tonight to hang out.
*mo-YA **GYORL-frend** se-VOD-nya pri-DYOT po-ob-SCHAT-sya.*
Моя **гёрлфренд** сегодня придёт пообщаться.
Sometimes you might hear this shortened to гёрла (*GYOR-la*).

You're the best lover (male) I've ever had.
*ti SA-mii LU-chshii **lyu-BOV-nik**, ko-TO-rii u me-NYA kog-DA-LI-bo bil.*
Ты самый лучший **любовник**, который у меня когда-либо был.

The whole time they were married, he had a lover (female) on the side.
*vsyo VRE-mya, kog-DA o-NI BI-li zhen-A-ti, u nye-VO bil-A **lyu-BOV-nitsa** na sto-ro-NYE.*
Всё время, когда они были женаты, у него была **любовница** на стороне.

I just can't seem to forget my old flame.
*ya ni-KAK nye mo-GU za-BIT svo-YU **bIV-shu-yu PA-ssi-yu**.*
Я никак не могу забыть свою **бывшую пассию**.

I met my fiancée through the internet.
*ya po-zna-KO-mil-sya so svo-YEI **ne-VYE-stoi** CHE-rez in-ter-NET.*
Я познакомился со своей **невестой** через Интернет.
Russians use невеста for both "fiancée" and "bride" and жених for both "fiancé" and "groom."

My fiancé and I just registered at ZAGS.
*mi s mo-IM **zhe-ni-KHOM** TOL-ko chto za-re-gi-STRI-ro-va-lis v ZAG-sye.*
Мы с моим **женихом** только что зарегистрировались в ЗАГСе.
Couples in Russia are officially engaged once they've registered at this Soviet-style marriage hall. This is also where the civil ceremony takes place.

·····Acquaintances, coworkers, and enemies
zna-KO-mi-ye, so-TRUD-ni-ki, i vra-GI
Знакомые, сотрудники, и враги

Who is that guy?
*chto za **CHE-lik**?*
Что за **челик**?

What's that chick's name?
*kak E-tu **dev-CHON-ku** zo-VUT?*
Как эту **девчонку** зовут?

All broads are wenches.
*vsye **BA-bi**—STYER-vi.*
Все **бабы**—стервы.
Hey, it's just a song.

This acquaintance of mine once hitchhiked from Moscow to Irkutsk.
*o-DIN moi **zna-KO-mii** od-NA-zhdi YE-khal av-to-STOP-om ot mosk-VI do ir-KUTSK-a.*
Один мой **знакомый** однажды ехал автостопом от Москвы до Иркутска.

I never give my phone number to strangers.
*ya ni-kog-DA nye da-YU svoi NO-mer te-le-FO-na **ne-zna-KOM-tsam**.*
Я никогда не даю свой номер телефона **незнакомцам**.

My coworkers are a bunch of morons.
*vsye mo-I **so-TRUD-ni-ki**—pri-DUR-ki.*
Все мои **сотрудники**—придурки.

TERMS OF ENDEARMENT)))
LA-SKO-VI-YE SLO-VA
ЛАСКОВЫЕ СЛОВА

Dear (male/female)
do-ro-GOI/do-ro-GA-ya
Дорогой/дорогая

Dearie
do-ro-GU-sha
Дорогуша

My honey (male/female)
moi MI-len-kii/mo-YA MI-len-ka-ya
Мой миленький/моя миленькая

My better half
mo-YA LUCH-sha-ya po-lo-VIN-ka
Моя лучшая половинка

My sweetie (male/female)
moi lyu-BIM-chik/mo-YA lyu-BIM-itsa
Мой любимчик/моя любимица

Sunshine
SOL-nish-ko
Солнышко

My love!
lyu-BOV mo-YA!
Любовь моя!

Hunny bunny
ZAI-ka
Зайка

My sweetie pie
moi PUP-sik
Мой пупсик

My little cutie
mo-YA LA-poch-ka
Моя лапочка

My colleagues and I are here on a business trip.
*mi so svo-I-mi **ko-LLYE-ga-mi** zdyes v ko-mman-dir-O-vkye.*
Мы со своими **коллегами** здесь в командировке.

Their CEO was arrested last week for fraud.
*ikh **GYE-na** bil a-rest-O-van na PRO-shloi nye-DYEL-ye za mo-SHE-ni-chest-vo.*
Их **гена** был арестован на прошлой неделе за мошенничество.

My boss pays me under the table.
*moi **shef** mnye PLA-tit pod stol-OM.*
Мой **шеф** мне платит под столом.

My supervisor cussed me out for being late.
moi na-CHAL-nik me-NYA ot-ru-GAL za o-po-ZDA-ni-ye.
Мой **начальник** меня отругал за опоздание.

My manager is sleeping with his secretary.
moi MA-na-ger spit so svo-YEI se-kre-TAR-shei.
Мой **манагер** спит со своей секретаршей.
This is the slangy pronunciation of менеджер (*ME-ne-dzher*).

The barista at the coffee shop is my arch nemesis.
E-ta ba-RI-sta v KO-fye KHAU-sye moi ko-VAR-nii vrag.

Boris is my mortal enemy.
bo-RIS—moi za-KLYA-tii vrag.
Борис—мой **заклятый враг**.
Эта бариста в кофе хаусе мой **коварный враг**.

·····Russian names
RU-sski-ye i-me-NA
Русские имена

Russian is a very expressive language, especially when it comes to names. They are several ways to address people by name depending on the degree of formality and the range of feelings you want to show to that person. In formal situations (where you would use *vy*), you generally address the person by name and patronymic. The patronymic is formed by the person's father's first name plus –ovich for a guy and –ovna for a chick.

In very official situations, Russians will often be asked to give their Ф.И.О. (FIO), which stands for фамилия-имя-отчество (*fa-MI-liya-I-mya-OT-che-stvo*): last name, first name, patronymic.

In more casual situations (one where you would use *ty*), usually the short version of the first name is used, and with close friends and loved ones, various diminutives will be used expressing a range of emotions.

For example, my daughter's full first name is Мирослава (*Miroslava*). In formal situations, she would be called Мирослава Игоревна (*Miroslava Igorevna*), her patronymic derived from her father's first name, Igor. Informally, she could be called either Мира (*Mira*) or Слава (*Slava*).

There are numerous diminutives that can be used affectionately:

Мирочка (*Mirochka*), Мируся (*Mirusia*), Мируня (*Mirusnya*), Мирунчик (*Mirunchik*), Мирусик (*Mirusik*), Мирусичка (*Mirusichka*), Мирусинка (*Mirusinka*)

Or, when she's screwing around, she's known pejoratively as:

Мирка
Mirka

If I'm addressing her directly, I will call:

Эй, Мир!
Hey, Mir!
This is something of a new vocative whereby the short form of a name ending in a loses its ending when you are directly addressing the person.

For a guy, it's basically the same story. For example, my husband's name is Игорь (*Igor*). Formally, he would be Игорь Леонидович (*Igor Leonidovich*), and affectionately he could be called Игорёня (*Igoryonia*), or Игорёк (*Igoryok*).

All Russian names can do this, although there are some variations on endings depending on the name. But once you get the hang of it, you can really be as creative as you want—Russians certainly are!

·····Compliments
kom-pli-MYEN-ti
Комплименты

Even the gruffest of Russians can often be won over with a few kind words; however, they tend to be very sensitive to insincerity. So if you want to compliment a Russian, you better keep it real. Or better yet, follow it up with alcohol and chocolate.

You rock!
ti PRO-sto mo-lo-DYETS!
Ты просто молодец!
Molodyets is sort of an all-purpose compliment that can mean anything from "Good job" to "You're a swell guy."

Smartypants!
ti UM-nich-ka!
Ты умничка!

That's a helluva idea!
E-to SU-per-ska-ya i-DYE-ya!
Это суперская идея!

That's genius!
E-to ge-ni-AL-na-ya misl!
Это гениальная мысль!

Cool threads!
KLASS-ni-ye SHMOT-ki!
Классные шмотки!

I really dig...
ya PRO-sto bal-DYE-yu ot...
Я просто балдею от...
Note that this phrase is followed by the genitive case.

your **groovy** style.
*tvo-ye-VO **KLYO-vo-vo** STIL-ya.*
твоего **клёвого** стиля.

your **rad** hairstyle.
*tvo-YEI **o-bal-DYE-nnoi** pri-CHO-ski.*
твоей **обалденной** причёски.

your **trendy** jeans.
*tvo-IKH **MOD-nikh** JINS-ov.*
твоих **модных** джинсов.

your **slick** new **murse.**
*tvo-YEI **shi-KAR-noi** NO-voi **bar-SYET-ki.***
твоей **шикарной** новой **барсетки.**
In other words, a man purse.

your **amusing** (eye)glasses.
*tvo-IKH **pri-KOL-nikh** och-KOV.*
твоих **прикольных** очков.

You have **awesome** taste.
*u te-BYA **o-fig-YE-nnii** vkus.*
У тебя **офигенный** вкус.

You look really **cool.**
*ti **KLASS-no** VI-glyad-ish.*
Ты **классно** выглядишь.

You're dressed real **snazzy.**
*ti **a-TAS-no** o-DYET.*
Ты **атасно** одет.

You look **fly** in that dress.
*ti **KRU-to** VI-glyad-ish v E-tom PLA-tye.*
Ты **круто** выглядишь в этом платье.

She's a really **cool chick.**
*on-A **KLASS-na-ya** dyev-CHON-ka.*
Она **классная девчонка.**

He's an **awesome guy.**
*on **SLAV-nii PAR-en.***
Он **славный парень.**

I envy you.
ya te-BYE za-VID-u-yu.
Я тебе завидую.

In Russian, there are two kinds of envy: белая зависть
(*BYEL-a-ya ZA-vist*), or "white envy," and чёрная зависть
(*CHORN-a-ya ZA-vist*), or "black envy." White envy is
the good kind of envy where ultimately you are genuinely

happy for the person and their good fortune. Black envy, on the other hand, is the kind where you secretly wish the person would spontaneously combust right in front of you so that you could witness their suffering and death and then confiscate the object of your envy so that it can be yours, all yours.

·····Cool!
KLASS-no!
Классно!

Klassno is still the most common, basic way of saying "Cool!" It is also often shortened to класс (*klass*). Here a few others:

Rad!
a-TAS-no!
Атасно!

Groovy!
KLYO-vo!
Клёво!

That rules!
RUL-no!
Рульно!

Tight!
KRU-to!
Круто!

Fuckin' sweet!
piz-DA-to!
Пиздато!

Phat!
o-fi-GYEN-no!
Офигенно!

That's a hoot!
pri-LOL-no!
Прикольно!

Super!
SU-per!
Супер!

Awesome!
ZDO-ro-vo
Здорово!

As already mentioned, remember this is stressed *ZDO-ro-vo*, distinguishing it from the greeting *zdo-RO-vo*.

Now you're talkin'!
vot E-to da!
Вот это да!

It doesn't suck.
nye khren-O-ven-ko.
Не хреновенько.

·····Time for a little romance
po-RA dlya ro-MAN-ti-ki
Пора для романтики

Those long Russian nights can get a little lonely, so why not find someone who'll make the time fly by. Keep in mind that dating in Russia is a bit like dating during the Eisenhower years, but with more sex. Guys generally make all the moves and are expected to foot the bill. They're also expected to hold open doors, help put on coats, and offer a hand to assist their female companions out of cars—so be prepared to work if you're looking for a payoff. Oh, and if you decide to bring your girl flowers, make sure you buy an odd number—even-numbered bouquets are only for funerals, and that's probably not quite the message you want to send before an evening of romance.

To flirt
flirt-o-VAT
Флиртовать

I am really sick of guys always hitting on me at parties.
*mnye na-do-YE-lo, kak PAR-ni po-sto-YA-nno **pri-sta-YUT ko mnye** na ve-cher-IN-kakh.*
Мне надоело, как парни постоянно **пристают ко мне** на вечеринках.

Where can I pick up a chick/guy around here?
*gdye tut MO-zhno **snyat** TYOL-ku/PAR-nya?*
Где тут можно **снять** тёлку/парня?

Could I get your number?
MO-zhno tvoi te-le-FON-chik?
Можно твой телефончик?

What's your sign?
kto ti po zo-di-A-ku?
Кто ты по зодиаку?

Do you believe in love at first sight?
*ti VYER-ish v **lyu-BOV s PYER-vo-vo VZGLYA-da**?*
Ты веришь в **любовь с первого взгляда**?

I think we've met somewhere before.
po-MO-ye-mu, mi GDYE-to u-ZHE vstre-CHAL-is.
По-моему, мы где-то уже встречались.

My friend thinks you're really cute.
moi drug schi-TA-yet te-BYA O-chen sim-pa-TICH-noi.
Мой друг считает тебя очень симпатичной.

Can I buy you a drink?
MO-zhno te-BYA u-go-STIT chem-ni-BUD VI-pit?
Можно тебя угостить чем-нибудь выпить?

Hey, pretty lady, wanna get to know each other better?
pri-VYET, kra-SA-vi-tsa, KHO-chesh po-zna-KOM-it-sya po-BLI-zhe?
Привет, красавица, хочешь познакомиться поближе?

Are you free tonight?
ti svo-BOD-na se-VOD-nya VE-che-rom?
Ты свободна сегодня вечером?

Could you set me up on a blind date?
*yi bi nye mo-GLI mnye u-STRO-it **svi-DAN-i-ye vslyep-U-yu**?*
Вы бы не могли мне устроить **свидание вслепую**?

Let's make a plan, Fran (or Stan).
da-VAI za-BYOM STRYEL-ku.
Давай забьём стрелку.

Hey, honey, wanna go...?
eh, kra-SOT-ka, nye KHO-chesh po-i-TI...?
Эй, красотка, не хочешь пойти...?

> **on a date**
> *na svi-DAN-i-ye*
> на свидание

> **back to my place**
> *ko mnye do-MOI*
> ко мне домой

> **to the movies tonight**
> *se-VOD-nya v ki-NO*
> сегодня в кино

> **to a dance club**
> *na dis-KACH*
> на дискач

> **to a new club with me**
> *so mnoi v NO-vii klub*
> со мной в новый клуб

·····Characters
per-so-NA-zhi
Персонажи

It takes all kinds, and Russia is full of 'em! Here are of some of the many people you run the risk of meeting on the wild streets of Moscow.

> **He thinks he's a total badass because he rides a motorcycle.**
> *on schi-TA-yet se-BYA **kru-TIM PAR-nyem**, po-to-MU chto YEZ-dit na mo-to-TSI-klye.*
> Он считает себя **крутым парнем**, потому что ездит на мотоцикле.

That **moocher** always shows up around dinnertime.
*E-tot **kha-LYAV-schik** vseg-DA pri-KHO-dit k U-zhin-u.*
Этот **халявщик** всегда приходит к ужину.

I know that **gigolo** is just using her for her money.
*ya ZNA-yu, chto E-tot **al-FONS** ye-YO i-SPOL-zu-yet PRO-sto RA-di DYEN-yeg.*
Я знаю, что этот **альфонс** её использует просто ради денег.

That **jezebel** ruined his life.
*E-ta **di-na-MIST-i-ka** is-POR-ti-la ye-MU zhizn.*
Эта **динамистка** испортила ему жизнь.

That **old geezer** spends his pension on vodka.
*E-tot **sta-ri-CHOK** TRA-tit svo-YU PYEN-si-yu na VOD-ku.*
Этот **старичок** тратит свою пенсию на водку.

Because of these **old farts**, there's nowhere to sit on the tram.
*IZ-za E-tikh **star-PYOR-ov** v tram-VA-ye NYE-gdye syest.*
Из-за этих **старпёров** в трамвае негде сесть.

Those **old biddies** are always gossiping about me in the stairwell.
*E-ti **sta-RU-khi** po-sto-YA-nno SPLYET-ni-cha-yut obo MNYE v pod-YEZ-dye.*
Эти **старухи** постоянно сплетничают обо мне в подъезде.

I'm looking for a **sugar daddy**.
*ya i-SCHU se-BYE **SPON-so-ra**.*
Я ищу себе **спонсора**.

Even though he's married, he's still an incurable **skirt chaser**.
*nye-smo-TRYA na TO, chto zhe-NAT, on **BAB-nik** nye-iz-le-CHI-mii.*
Несмотря на то, что женат, он **бабник** неизлечимый.

That **old maid** still lives with her mother.
*E-ta **STAR-a-ya DYE-va** do sikh POR zhi-VYOT so svo-YEI MA-ter-yu.*
Эта **старая дева** до сих пор живёт со своей матерью.

In Russia, an old maid is basically any woman who's over 25 and still single.

Thirtysomething woman

ZHEN-schi-na bal-ZA-kov-sko-vo VO-zrast-a

Женщина бальзаковского возраста

If you want to know more about what this is, there's actually a popular Russian TV show of the same name. It's basically a takeoff of "Sex and the City," only Muscofied.

I would never marry a mama's boy.

*ya bi ni-kog-DA nye VI-shla ZA-muzh za **MA-min-kin-a si-NOCH-ka***.

Я бы никогда не вышла замуж за **маминкина сыночка**.

That daddy's girl always wears Gucci.

*E-ta **PA-pin-kin-a DOCH-ka** vseg-DA NO-sit GU-chi.*

Эта **папинкина дочка** всегда носит Гуччи.

My little brother is such a snotty kid.

*moi MLAD-shii brat—**MA-lyen-kii chpok***.

Мой младший брат—**маленький чпок**.

I almost shat myself when I found out that she's jailbait.

*ya chut ne ob-o-SRAL-sya kog-DA uz-NAL, chto on-A **ma-lo-LYET-ka***.

Я чуть не обосрался когда узнал, что она **малолетка**.

My teenage friends are always slacking off after school.

*mo-I dru-ZYA-**ti-NEi-je-ri** vseg-DA byez-DYEL-ni-cha-yut PO-sle SHKOL-i.*

Мои друзья-**тинэйджеры** всегда бездельничают после школы.

This energizer bunny goes jogging every morning.

*E-tot **e-ner-JAi-zer** KAZH-do-ye U-tro na pro-BYEZH-kye.*

Этот **энерджайзер** каждое утро на пробежке.

That computer geek is always wrapped up in his programs.

*tot **kom-PYU-ter-schik** po-sto-YA-nno za-vi-SA-yet za pro-GRA-mma-mi.*

Тот **компьютерщик** постоянно зависает за программами.

That **gamer** never leaves his comp.
*E-tot **GEI-mer** ot komp-A nye ot-KHO-dit.*
Этот **геймер** от компа не отходит.

There were a bunch of drunk **rockers** at the concert last night.
*BI-lo SBOR-i-sche PYAN-ikh **RO-ker-ov** vche-RA na kon-TSER-tye.*
Было сборище пьяных **рокеров** вчера на концерте.

Do you know where I can meet some local **punks**?
*ti nye ZNA-yesh, gdye MO-zhno po-zna-KOM-it-sya s MYEST-ni-mi **PANK-a-mi**?*
Ты не знаешь, где можно познакомиться с местными **панками**?

That **hippie** walks around barefoot all day.
*E-tot **KHI-ppi** KHO-dit TSE-lii dyen bo-si-KOM.*
Этот **хиппи** ходит целый день босиком.

I think that **skin** is a follower of Barkashov.
*po-MO-ye-mu E-tot **skin** DRU-zhit s bar-ka-SHOV-im.*
По-моему этот **скин** сторонник Баркашова.
Alexander Barkashov is the former leader of the radical nationalist political group RNE (Russian National Unity), which attracted a lot of skinhead followers based on its agenda of ridding Russia of "foreigners and Jews."

Those damned **bikers** are causing problems again.
*E-ti pro-KLYA-ti-ye **BAI-ke-ri** o-PYAT pro-BLYE-mi so-zda-YUT.*
Эти проклятые **байкеры** опять проблемы создают.

That **hick** has never seen nothin' but dung.
*E-tot **kol-KHOZ-nik** KRO-mye na-VO-za ni-che-VO v ZHIZ-ni nye VI-dyel.*
Этот **колхозник** кроме навоза ничего в жизни не видел.
Literally, this means "collective farmer" but can describe any country-bumpkin type.

Posers really annoy me.
***PO-ze-ri** me-NYA O-chen raz-dra-ZHA-yut.*
Позеры меня очень раздражают.
Another variant of this word is позёр (*po-ZYOR*).

That **slacker** just goofs off all day.

*E-tot **byez-DYEL-nik** TSE-lii dyen za-ni-MA-ye-tsya ye-run-DOI.*

Этот **бездельник** целый день занимается ерундой.

I can't believe how many **bums** there are in Moscow!

*nye mo-GU VYER-it, STOL-ko yest **bom-ZHEI** v mosk-VYE!*

Не могу поверить, столько есть **бомжей** в Москве!

He's a three-time **loser**.

*on TRIZH-di **nye-u-DACH-nik**.*

Он трижды **неудачник**.

Although the English word "loser" (лузер) has also arisen in recent years.

That ***hooligan*** jacked my wallet!

*E-tot **khu-li-GAN** SPIZ-dil moi ko-shel-OK!*

Этот **хулиган** спиздил мой кошелёк!

This is the general Russian term describing anyone from a loudmouthed drunk to a gangbanger.

No one respects **the cops** in Russia.

*ni-KTO nye u-va-ZHA-yet **myent-OV** v ro-SSII.*

Никто не уважает **ментов** в России.

•••••Only in Russia

TOL-ko v ro-SSII

Только в России

New Russian

NO-vii RU-sskii

Новый русский

These are the guys who made a whole lotta dough on dubious business ventures and now drive around in expensive *inomarki*, own sweet dachas in *podmoskovie*, vacation in Ibiza, and yet still talk like the Russian version of Rocky Balboa. Their offspring are sometimes referred to as the Золотая молодёжь (*zo-lo-TA-ya mo-lo-DYOZH*), or "Golden youth."

That **New Russian** has a bitchin' black Beemer.

*u E-to-vo **NO-vo-vo RU-ssko-vo** kru-TOI CHOR-nii BU-mer.*

У этого **нового русского** крутой чёрный бумер.

Bandit

ban-DIT
Бандит

Bandits are pretty much the same as New Russians, just less successful and with fewer pretenses of respectability.

> **Odessa used to be known as a bandit's city.**
> *o-DYE-ssa RAN-she bi-LA iz-VYEST-na kak **ban-DIT-skii** GOR-od.*
> Одесса раньше была известна как **бандитский** город.

Russian intellectual

in-tye-lli-GYENT
Интеллигент

There's really no exact English equivalent for this word. It's similar to an intellectual, but one with particular interest in moral and social issues, often devoted to defending against the degradation of high culture and placing great importance on behaving in a proper manner. They are the polar opposite of the *noviye russkiye* and tend to feel a smug sense of moral superiority that is heightened by the abject poverty in which they often live. Nevertheless, интеллигентный (*in-tye-lli-GYENT-nii*) is just about the highest compliment you can give to a Russian over the age of 25.

> **That intellectual likes to sit in the kitchen all night and discuss philosophy.**
> *E-tot **in-tye-lli-GYENT** LYU-bit si-DYET vsyu NOCH na KUKH-nye i ra-ssu-ZHDAT o fi-lo-SO-fii.*
> Этот **интеллигент** любит сидеть всю ночь на кухне и рассуждать о философии.

There's this whole thing in Russian culture, sometimes called "kitchen talk," where people (most often *intelligyenti*) sit in the kitchen all night and pontificate on the ills of society.

Sovok

so-VOK
Совок

This term refers to someone with a Soviet mentality, and generally not in a complimentary way. These folks tend to spend most of their time complaining about capitalism and waxing nostalgic about Russia's former glory as a superpower. You can usually find them eating *shproty* under a portrait of Lenin in some rundown *kommunalka*, or complaining about the price of bread at any Soviet-style *produkty* store.

That **sovok** thinks that all foreigners are CIA secret agents.
E-tot so-VOK DU-ma-yet, chto VSYE i-no-STRAN-tsi—TAI-ni-ye a-GYEN-ti tse-er-U.
Этот **совок** думает, что все иностранцы—тайные агенты ЦРУ.

Mazhor
Ma-ZHOR
Мажор

The spoiled son of an influential and/or wealthy man. They pretty much get a free pass in life since *papochka* can always use his connections down at the ministry to get them out of any jam.

> He's just a fucking **mazhor** whose daddy always pays his way.
> *on YO-ba-nnii ma-ZHOR, ko-TO-rii zhi-VYOT za PA-pin schot.*
> Он ёбаный **мажор**, который живёт за папин счёт.

Pofigist
po-fig-IST
Пофигист

Someone who just doesn't give a shit about anything.

> That **pofigist** sleeps all day because he doesn't see the point of getting up.
> *E-tot po-fig-IST TSE-li-mi DNYA-mi spit, po-to-MU chto ne VI-dit SMI-sla vsta-VAT.*
> Этот **пофигист** целыми днями спит, потому что не видит смысла вставать.

Thug
GOP-nik
Гопник

A *gopnik* is a Russian thug. He spends his time drinking vodka out of plastic cups and spitting sunflower seed shells all over the sidewalk on which he tends to squat. There seem to be fewer of them these days in Moscow, but there is no shortage out in the provinces.

> Only **thugs** party at that club.
> *v E-tom KLU-bye tu-SU-yu-tsya TOL-ko GOP-ni-ki.*
> В этом клубе тусуются только **гопники**.

Ex-con
zek
Зек

This is the former inmate of a prison camp, and the term comes from the abbreviation for заключённый каналоармеец. Probably the easiest way to spot a *zek* is by his tattoos: Although his tats have become popular in recent years among young people, they were traditionally a part of prison culture in Russia. Prison tats, however, usually involve coded symbols that, if correctly interpreted, can tell you which crimes the person has committed and what kind of time he served, among other interesting biographical facts.

Judging by his tattoos, he's an ex-con.
*SU-dya po ye-VO ta-tu-ir-OV-kam, on—**zek**.*
Судя по его татуировкам, он—**ЗЭК**.

·····Student life
stu-DYEN-ches-ka-ya zhizn
Студенческая жизнь

The Russian academic year is divided into two parts, called сессия (*sEssiya*): зимняя сессия (*ZIM-nya-ya SYE-ssi-ya*) and весенняя сессия (*vye-SYE-nya-ya SYE-ssi-ya*). Each *sessiya* is followed by an exam period called экзаменационная сессия (*ek-za-men-a-tsi-ONN-ay-a SYE-ssi-ya*). Russian doesn't really have words for freshman, sophomore, etc.; instead, they just say на первом курсе (*na PYER-vom KUR-sye*), на втором курсе (*na vto-ROM KUR-sye*), and so on.

High school education through 9th grade
nye-POL-no-ye SRYED-ne-ye o-bra-zo-VA-ni-ye
Неполное среднее образование
After 9th grade you have the option of leaving school and learning a trade. Or just smoking pot all day.

High school education through 11th grade
POL-no-ye SRYED-ne-ye o-bra-zo-VA-ni-ye
Полное среднее образование
Russian secondary schools go through 11 grades, so this is someone who has completed his secondary education and actually harbors some ambition in life.

Any educational institute beyond high school
VUZ
ВУЗ
This is the abbreviation for высшее учебное заведение (*VI-sshe-ye u-CHEB-no-ye za-ve-DYE-ni-ye*), which means

something like institute of higher learning and refers to anything post–high school.

Vo-tech
peh-teh-U
ПТУ
This stands for Профессионально-техническое училище (*pro-fye-ssi-o-NAL-no-tyekh-NI-che-sko-ye u-CHI-li-sche*) and is usually for the kids not really cut out for schoolin'.

Those vo-tech students just drink beer all day.
E-ti pe-te-U-shni-ki TOL-ko PI-vo pyut TSEL-ii dyen.
Эти пэтэушники только пиво пьют целый день.

College
KO-llej
Колледж
A college is considered less prestigious than a университет (*u-ni-vyer-si-TYET*), or university.

Uni
u-ni-VYER
Универ
This abbreviated form is often used informally.

Grad school
a-spi-ran-TU-ra
Аспирантура

You'll never get into **grad school** with those grades!
*ti ni-kog-DA nye po-STU-pish v **a-spi-ran-TU-ru** s ta-KI-mi o-TSEN-ka-mi!*
Ты никогда не поступишь в **аспирантуру** с такими оценками!

Getting a grade for a class without needing to take a final exam
av-to-MAT
Автомат

I got an A **without taking the final.**
*ya po-lu-CHIL pya-TYOR-ku **av-to-MAT-om.***
Я получил пятёрку **автоматом**.

By the way, the Russian grading system is a five-point scale. A 5 is called a пятёрка (*pya-TYOR-ka*) and is the equivalent of an A. It goes down from there. A 4 is a четвёрка (*chet-VYOR-ka*); a 3 is a тройка (*TROI-ka*) and is the lowest grade you can get and still pass. A 2 is a двойка (*DVOI-ka*) and is a falling grade. A 1 is essentially never given unless a teacher has a real personal grudge against a student.

Study nerd
bo-TAN
Ботан
Short for ботаник (*bo-TAN-ik*).

Total slacker student
stye-RIL-nii
Стерильный
This is the opposite of the ботан. He just always comes unprepared and has, on some level, accepted his fate as a failure.

The very first semester of one's college career
bo-ye-VO-ye kre-SCHE-ni-ye
Боевое крещение
The more standard meaning of this funny, slangy term is "baptism by fire."

The halfway mark in your college degree program
ek-VA-tor
Экватор

Cheat sheet
SHPOR-a
Шпора
Short for шпаргалка (*shpar-GAL-ka*).

Cheat sheet
BOM-ba
Бомба
This kind of cheat sheet has answers to the exact questions on the test.

Student ticket
stu-DAK
Студак
Short for студенческий билет (*stu-DYEN-ches-kii bi-LYET*). When Russian students take exams, they must randomly draw a "ticket." Whatever question is written on the ticket is what they must answer for their final exam grade. Unless their parents have a lot of money.

•••••The Russian army
ro-SSII-ska-ya AR-mi-ya
Российская армия

Russia still has a mandatory draft that just about everyone tries to avoid by any means possible, including bribing a doctor to write a medical exemption, checking into a mental institute, going to college and/or grad school, or just plain running away. It's hard to blame them: Aside from the history of numerous and deadly military adventures in the Caucasus, Russian soldiers live in deplorable conditions and face a kind of military hazing that is beyond cruel and unusual. But if you don't have the brains or the connections to get yourself out of service, then once you turn 18, you're pretty much stuck waiting for your number to come up. Not surprisingly, the suicide rate is quite high.

He signed himself into the nuthouse to dodge the draft.
*on za-pi-SAL-sya v dur-DOM, CHTO-bi **u-klon-YAT-sya ot pri-ZI-va**.*
Он записался в дурдом, чтобы **уклоняться от призыва**.

The recruit started playing the crazy card as soon as they tried to send him to Chechnya.
*no-vo-BRA-nyets **NA-chal ko-SIT pod du-ra-KA**, kak TOL-ko ye-VO sta-RA-lis po-SLAT v chech-NYU.*
Новобранец **начал косить под дурака**, как только его старались послать в Чечню.

The soldier snuck out to get some booze.
*sol-DAT **u-SHOL v sa-mo-VOL-ku** za VI-piv-koi.*
Солдат **ушёл в самоволку** за выпивкой.

Samovolka is essentially going AWOL but usually only for a brief period of time, such as to make a quick vodka run.

GI
o-bye-ZYA-na
Обезьяна
Literally, a monkey

A fellow soldier from your hometown
ZYO-ma
Зёма

A recruit in his first year of service
dukh
Дух

A recruit in his second and final year
dyed
Дед
Hence the following word for "hazing."

There's crazy hazing in the Russian army.
*v ro-SSII-skoi AR-mii po-VAL-na-ya **dye-dov-SCHI-na**.*
В российской армии повальная **дедовщина**.

Combat boots
BYER-tsi
Берцы

His puttees really reek!
*ye-VO **por-TYAN-ki** U-zhas kak vo-NYA-yut!*
Его **портянки** ужас как воняют!
In case you don't know, puttees are those nasty foot cloths
soldiers wear instead of socks.

Chow
bol-TI
Болты
Specifically, this is pearl barley kasha, which is pretty much all
Russian soldiers are ever given to eat.

MIA
vpro-YO-bye
Впроёбе
Not so much in the literal sense of disappearing in combat; more
like just "whereabouts unknown."

KIA (killed in action)
dvukh-SO-tii
Двухсотый

WIA (wounded in action)
tryokh-SO-tii
Трёхсотый

Military prison
gaupt-VAKH-ta
Гауптвахта

The brig
gu-BA
Губа

Don't screw around with the Special Forces.
nad **spyets-NA-zom** *nye iz-dye-VAI-sya.*
Над **спецназом** не издевайся.
These guys are the real badasses of the Russian military.

He who serves in the army doesn't laugh at the circus.
kto v AR-mii slu-ZHIL, tot v TSIR-kye nye sme-YO-tsya.
Кто в армии служил, тот в цирке не смеётся.
A famous army proverb about the absurdities of army life.

A lot Afghan vets live in fucking awful conditions.
MNO-gi-ye **af-GAN-tsi** *zhi-VUT v khu-YO-vikh u-SLO-vi-yakh.*
Многие **Афганцы** живут в хуёвых условиях.
In many ways, Afghanistan was for the Soviet Union what Vietnam was for America, and there are a whole lotta vets in Russia missing eyes and limbs, sometimes homeless, and often of questionable mental stability. They are now being joined by the new generation of Chechen war veterans who are in pretty much the same condition upon their return to the Motherland. Aside from old people selling off all of their possessions for a few kopecks to buy bread, this is probably one of the saddest things you'll ever see in Russia.

Also, an abbreviation you will often see is ВОВ (*VOV*), which stands for Великая отечественная война (*ve-LI-ka-ya o-TYE-chyest-vye-nna-ya voi-NA*), the Great Patriotic War. This is what Russians call World War II, and if you know anything about the astronomical losses the Soviet Union suffered, you'll understand why it holds a sacred place in Russia's historical memory. However, unless you are willing to admit that Russia won the war single-handedly, this is probably a topic best avoided.

CHAPTER 3

PARTY RUSSIAN

TU-SO-VOCH-NII RU-SKII
Тусовочный русский

The legends of Russian drinking are not exaggerated: Russians are hard-core drinkers, and bacchanalian revelry pervades all aspects of life from the quick beer on the way to work to liquid lunches and vodka-drenched business meetings to all-night parties that rapidly degenerate into a marathon of reckless bingeing, blurring all lines between Friday night and Monday morning into a foggy haze of excess and regret. Let's face it: If you hang with Russians, you will drink. A lot. And in all likelihood at the most inappropriate times and in the most inappropriate places.

·····Tying one on
o-pya-NYE-ni-ye
Опьянение

Let's go...
poi-DYOM...
Пойдём...

> **for a drink.**
> *VI-pit.*
> выпить.

SBITEN

Ain't no party like a Genghis Khan party, cuz a Genghis Khan party don't stop. Russians have been drinking this warm concoction of honey, spices, and booze since the 12th century. A big batch is certain to heat things up.

GET THESE:

½ cup honey
1 teaspoon whole cloves
3 cinnamon sticks
1 teaspoon ground ginger
8 ounces blackberry jam
2 (750-ml) bottles red wine
¼ teaspoon ground nutmeg
2 tablespoons chopped mint leaves
2 whole dried chili peppers
1 cup vodka or brandy (optional)

DO THIS:

In a medium saucepan, combine the honey, cloves, cinnamon sticks, ginger, blackberry jam, wine, and nutmeg, along with the mint leaves and chili peppers. Slowly bring the mixture to a low simmer over medium heat, stirring frequently until the honey and jam completely dissolve. Remove from the heat right away; do not let it boil! Let the sbiten come to room temperature. Strain the liquid through a cheesecloth, pressing on the solids, and transfer to an airtight container or back into the wine bottles. Refrigerate, reheat, and top off with the optional vodka or brandy. Then serve it up to your pack of party animals.

drinkin'.
po-DRINK-at.
подринкать.
From the English word "drink." There is also a noun form, дринк (*drink*).

boozing.
DYOR-nem.
дёрнем.

really tie one on.
po-bu-KHAT.
побухать.

drink some booze.
bu-KHAT bu-KHASH-ku.
бухать бухашку.

party.
za-zhi-GAT.
зажигать.

do some drinkin'.
BAKH-nut.
бахнуть.

wet our whistles.
na-ka-TIT.
накатить.

get hammered.
bukh-NYOM.
бухнём.

get smashed.
na-ZHRYOM-sya.
нажрёмся.

I need a drink.
kho-CHU VI-pit.
Хочу выпить.

I want to get drunk.
kho-CHU na-PIT-sya.
Хочу **напиться**.

I'm jonesing for a drink.
TRU-bi gor-YAT.
Трубы горят.

Pour 'em!
na-li-VAI!
Наливай!

Let me get this round.
da-VAI ya za-bosh-LYA-yu.
Давай я **забошляю**.

I demand that the banquet continue!
ya TRYE-bu-yu pro-dol-ZHE-ni-ya ban-KYE-ta!
Я требую продолжения банкета!
Score some cultural points with this famous line from the classic Soviet comedy Иван Васильевич меняет профессию (Ivan Vasilievich Changes Professions).

·····Where Russians get drunk
gdye RU-sski-ye na-pi-VA-yu-tsya
Где русские напиваются

Russians drink everywhere. Bars and clubs are all around,
from dives hidden away in piss-soaked basements to
upscale establishments full of flat-headed thugs in leather
jackets and bouncers checking weapons at the door.
When in Russia, choose your watering hole wisely!

Let's go...
poi-DYOM...
Пойдём...
Remember when talking about direction, you need to use the
accusative case.

to a bar.
v bar.
в бар.

to a club.
v klub.
в клуб.

to a dance club.
na dis-ko-TYE-ku.
на дискотеку.

to a disco.
na dis-KACH.
на дискач.

to a strip joint.
na strip-TIZ.
на стриптиз.

to a drinking party.
na PYAN-ku.
на пьянку.

to a booze bash.
na bu-KHA-lo-vo.
на бухалово.

to my place.
ko MNYE.
ко мне.

Let's drink…
da-VAi VI-pyem…
Давай выпьем…

> **on the street.**
> *na U-li-tse.*
> на улице.

> **in a park.**
> *v PAR-kye.*
> в парке.

> **in a stairwell.**
> *v pod-YEZ-dye.*
> в подъезде.

> **with some hos I know.**
> *u zna-KOM-ikh BLYA-dyei.*
> у знакомых блядей.

There's going to be a rockin' party tonight.
*se-VOD-nya BU-dyet KLASS-na-ya **tu-SOV-ka**.*
Сегодня будет классная **тусовка**.

Me and my buds are going for a guys' night out.
*mi so svo-I-mi re-BYA-ta-mi i-DYOM na **mal-CHISH-nik**.*
Мы со своими ребятами идём на **мальчишник**.

My girlfriend went to a hen party tonight while I sat at home like an idiot.
*po-KA ya TU-po si-DYEL DO-ma, mo-YA DYEV-ush-ka po-SHLA na **dyev-ICH-nik**.*
Пока я тупо сидел дома, моя девушка пошла на **девичник**.

The night is young.
VRE-mya DYET-sko-ye.
Время детское.

·····Booze
bu-KHLO
Бухло

Not surprisingly, the Russian drink of choice is vodka, most often shot straight up. Beer is becoming increasingly popular with the younger crowd, however, and many bars now offer both local and imported brews on tap.

Since Russia is all in love with the stupid metric system, you order vodka in measurements of 50 grams, which is just about two ounces (a typical American shot is an ounce and a half). So you can order as little as one small 50-gram drink (пятьдесят грамм) or—more likely—a 500-gram bottle (пол-литра). The standard shot, however, is 100 grams (сто грамм), sometimes just called a стопка (STOP-ka). For beer, you order by the parts of a liter—most commonly a third (called ноль три) or a half (called ноль пять), and you can actually buy up to 2.5 liters of beer in big plastic bottles as if it were soda. This is called a базука (ba-ZU-ka).

What are we having?
chto BU-dyem?
Что будем?

I'll have...
ya BU-du...
Я буду...
Notice that all of these words are in the accusative case.

vodka.
VOD-ku.
водку.

voddy.
VO-doch-ku.
водочку.
An affectionate term for vodka. You may also here the term водяра (*vo-DYAR-a*).

moonshine.
sa-mo-GON.
самогон.
Although the real sots just call this Russian homebrew сэм (*sem*).

pure grain alcohol.
chi-sto-GAN.
чистоган.

CHASERS)))

ZA-KU-SO-NI
ЗАКУСОНЫ

The Russian idea of a chaser is a lot more liberal than the American version. Although chasing vodka with fruit juice is possible, pounding down *sto gramm* will be followed more often by a swig of beer, by a bite of a pickle, or by sniffing a piece of black bread. It'll burn at first, but much to your own undoing, it'll get easier with each passing shot.

What can I **chase** with?
chem za-ku-SIT?
Чем закусить?

What can I **take a whiff of** (to kill the burn)?
chem za-NYU-khat?
Чем занюхать?

Let's **chase this vodka with some beer**.
da-VAI shli-fo-NYOM-sya.
Давай шлифонёмся.

cognac.
ko-NYAK.
коньяк.
The more slangy word is конина (*ko-NI-na*). This is, of course, more often brandy than actual cognac.

some brew.
piv-KO.
пивко.

yorsh.
yorsh.
ёрш.

A mixed drink consisting of vodka and beer.

beer and sour cream.
PI-vo so smye-TA-noi.
пиво со сметаной.
Before there was Viagra, there was beer and sour cream.

a little vino.
vin-TSO.
винцо.

mulled wine.
glint-VYEIN.
глинтвейн.

port.
port-VEIN.
портвейн.
It's cheap, it's potent, and it's also sometimes called
портвешок (*port-ve-SHOK*).

home-brewed fruit wine.
GRU-shki-YA-bloch-ki.
грушки-яблочки.

bubbly.
sham-PUN.
шамнунь.
Although it literally means "shampoo," so it's all about the
context here.

a cocktail.
kok-TYEIL.
коктейль.

a screwdriver.
ot-VYOR-ku.
отвёртку.

a bloody Mary.
kro-VA-vu-yu ME-ri.
кровавую Мэри.

a gin and tonic.
dzhin TO-nik.
джин тоник.

a rum and Coke.
rom KO-lu.
ром колу.

Do you have (dark, light) beer on tap?
*YEST u vas (TYOM-no-ye, SVYET-lo-ye) PI-vo **na roz-LI-vye**?*
Есть у вас (тёмное, светлое) пиво **на розливе**?

It's time to move on to something stronger.
*po-RA **pod-NYAT GRA-dus**.*
Пора **поднять градус**.

That bartender mixes a mean drink.
*E-tot bar-MEN **ba-DYA-zhit** KLASS-ni-ye kok-TYEI-li*
Этот бармен **бадяжит** классные коктейли.

Do you have anything stronger?
*YEST u vas chto-ni-BUD **po-KRYEP-che**?*
Есть у вас что-нибудь **покрепче**?

We'll drink anything that burns.
mi pyom VSYO, chto go-RIT.
Мы пьём всё, что горит.

They pour crap here.
tut na-li-VA-yut ta-KU-yu dryan.
Тут наливают такую **дрянь**.

I'm not going to drink this shitty beer.
ya nye BU-du pit E-to pi-zdo-VA-to-ye PI-vo.
Я не буду пить это **пиздоватое** пиво.

This is crappy vodka.
E-ta VOD-ka khre-NO-va-ya.
Эта водка **хреновая**.

After drinking that voddy, we were zonked.
PO-sle E-toi vo-DYA-ri mi Bl-li v A-u-tye.
После этой водяры мы были **в ауте**.

This home brew really packs a punch.
E-tot sem da-YOT ZHA-ru.
Этот сэм **даёт жару**.

That's a chick drink.
E-to BAB-skii na-PI-tok.
Это **бабский напиток**.

Let's each have a brew.
da-VAI po piv-KU.
Давай **по пивку**.

Let's have another round.
da-VAI e-SCHO po od-NOI.
Давай **ещё по одной**.

What, have you lost your fucking mind?!?! We've already drunk half a barrel!
ti CHTO, o-khu-YEL?!?! mi u-ZHE pol-BOCH-ki VI-pi-li!
Ты что, охуел?!?! Мы уже **полбочки** выпили!

Gimme some coin for beer.
go-NI mnye BAB-ki na PI-vo.
Гони мне **бабки** на пиво.

Give me some scratch.
dai ba-BLO.
Дай **бабло**.

SOME FINER POINTS OF RUSSIAN IMBIBING)))

Russians like to get the party started as quickly as possible, which means they waste no time pounding down the drinks. By tradition, the first shot is quickly followed by the second. A popular Russian saying goes:

> You don't take a break between the first and the second shots.
> *MYEZH-du PYER-voi i vto-ROI pye-rye-RIV-chik nye-bol-SHOI.*
> **Между первой и второй перерывчик небольшой.**

Keep in mind that Russian parties are a bit different from Americans parties. There is no mingling—hey, they didn't come to stand around making awkward small talk with a bunch of losers, they came to get shitfaced. When you go a Russian party, you sit, you eat, and you drink. *I vsyo.*

Down the hatch!
do DNA!
До дна!

This is generally how you'll be cheered on when pounding down shots.

A penalty drink
shtraf-NOI
Штрафной

So that any latecomers don't stay sober long enough to gather compromising information on their already shitfaced and loose-lipped companions.

Brudershaft
Брудершафт

This is a toast honoring the brotherhood of men in which you will be expected to link arms with guy next to you as you gaze deeply into each other's increasingly dilated pupils and pound down another shot. Bottoms up!

One for the road
na po-so-SHOK
На посошок

This is traditionally the last toast of the evening. Drink it down and get out while you still can!

And on a final note, there is a Russian custom of immediately removing empty bottles from the table. This often means placing them on the floor, under or beside the table. I'm not entirely sure why they do this: It may be superstition related, or it might just be a not-so-subtle hint that they are ready for another bottle to be opened.

·····Toasts
TOS-ti
Тосты

The more drunk Russians get, the longer and more tear-filled their toasts seem to be. But don't sweat it: It's not so much what you say, but the heart you put into it that will win over your drinking buddies. Most Russian toasts begin with variations of the following words:

Let's drink to...!
da-VAI VI-pyem za...!
Давай выпьем за...!

Here's to...!
da-VAI za...!¡¡
Давай за...!

> **meeting under the table.**
> *VSTRYE-chu pod sto-LOM.*
> встречу под столом.

> **women. We don't care what we drink to anyway, and it makes them happy.**
> *ZHEN-schin. NAM-to vsyo rav-NO, za CHTO pit, a IM-pri-YAT-no.*
> женщин. Нам-то всё равно, за что пить, а им-приятно.

> **a light heart and heavy pockets.**
> *LYO-gko-ye SYERD-tse i tya-ZHO-li-ye kar-MA-ni.*
> лёгкое сердце и тяжёлые карманы.

> **honest and humble people. There are so few of us left!**
> *CHYES-nikh i SKROM-nikh lyu-DYEI. nas o-STA-los tak MA-lo!*
> честных и скромных людей. Нас осталось так мало!

> **wives and lovers, and to them never meeting.**
> *zhon i lyu-BOV-nits, CHTO-bi on-i ni-kog-DA nye VSTRYE-ti-lis.*
> жён и любовниц, чтобы они никогда не встретились.

·····Wasted

bu-KHOI
Бухой

There will inevitably come a point where you're too drunk to slur out the words demanding another round. Not to worry: just do as the Russian do and flick your middle finger against the side of your neck. You'll have your *sto gramm* in no time!

He's/She's...
on/o-NA...
Он/она…

drunk.
PYA-nii/PYA-na-ya.
пьяный/пьяная.

a little tipsy.
slye-GKA pyan/pya-NA.
слегка пьян/пьяна.

shitfaced drunk.
v SRA-ku pyan/pya-NA.
в сраку пьян/пьяна.

drunk off his/her ass.
v ZHO-pu pyan/pyan-A.
в жопу пьян/пьяна.

completely wasted.
pyan/pya-nA v dro-VA.
пьян/пьяна в дрова.

wrecked.
pyan/pya-NA v khlam.
пьян/пьяна в хлам.

wasted.
bu-KHOI/bu-KHA-ya.
бухой/бухая.

already three sheets to the wind.
u-zZHE le-TA-yet.
уже летает.

feeling no pain.
kho-ROSH/kho-ro-SHA.
хорош/хороша.

on a bender.
v za-PO-ye.
в запое.

drinking like a Hussar.
pyot kak gu-SAR.
пьёт как гусар.
Which is apparently very fast.

I'm fucked up beyond all recognition.
mnye POL-nii piz-DYETS.
Мне полный пиздец.
This doesn't just refer to being drunk but can mean "I'm totally fucked" in just about any sense.

·····Drinkers
PYU-schi-ye
Пьющие

One thing it ain't hard to find in Russia is someone to drink with.

Drinking buddy
so-bu-TIL-nik
Собутыльник

A drunkard
PYA-ni-tsa
Пьяница

A total sot
A-lek
Алек

An alcoholic
al-ko-GO-lik
Алкоголик

A lousy, stinkin' lush
BU-khar
Бухарь

A boozer
si-NYAK
Синяк
This is also the word for "bruise"; it comes from синий (*SI-nii*), or "blue."

An alkie
al-KASH
Алкаш

That fucking alkie always wants to mooch drinks.
*E-tot **YO-ba-nnii al-KASH** vsyeg-DA KHO-chet na SHA-ru pit.*
Этот **ёбанный алкаш** всегда хочет на шару пить.

·····The cops
men-TI
Менты

Although public drunkenness is common in Russia, attracting too much attention to yourself could run you the risk of an unpleasant encounter with some of Russia's finest out trolling for a little supplementary income. Have your passport on hand, carry some spare cash, and practice saying these words so that you can express your righteous indignation the next day among your comrades.

Cops
men-TI
Менты

Pigs
MU-sor
Мусор
This what the real badasses call the po-po.

Po-po
lye-GA-vii
Легавый

The Fuzz
myen-TYA-ra
Ментяра

The pigs picked me up. Those bitches!
***mu-so-RA** me-NYA za-gre-BLI. SU-ki!*
Мусора меня загребли. Суки!

That new guy totally narc'ed me out to the **5-0**.
*E-tot gni-LOI me-NYA za-svye-TIL **dush-MA-nu**.*
Этот гнилой меня засветил **душману**.
This term is mainly used by druggies.

The cops made me pay a fine for being a public nuisance.
*men-TI za-STA-vi-li za-pla-TIT **shtraf** za khu-li-GAN-stvo.*
Менты заставили заплатить **штраф** за хулиганство.

"Fine" being a euphemism for what it really is:

A bribe
VZYAT-ka
Взятка

If you get caught with that shit, they'll send you up the river.
*YES-li ob-na-RU-zhit te-BYA s E-toi DRYA-nyu, to te-BYA po-SA-dyat na **kich-MAN**.*
Если обнаружат тебя с этой дрянью, то тебя посадят на **кичман**.

He did five years for possession.
*on si-DYEL pyat lyet za **khra-NYE-ni-ye**.*
Он сидел пять лет за **хранение**.

Russia is just completely whack.
*v ro-SSII POL-nii **byes-prye-DYEL**.*
В России полный **беспредел**.

Byespryedyel is a slang word right out of the big house now used to describe the chaotic lawlessness and corruption pervading Russian society.

·····The morning after
s u-tri-TSA
С утреца

If you don't find the following phrases useful after a night of gettin' your Russian groove on, then you ain't doin' it right.

I drank like a pig yesterday.
*ya vche-RA na-PIL-sya **kak svi-NYA**.*
Я вчера напился **как свинья**.

I made a real ass of myself.
ya o-po-ZO-ril-sya.
Я опозорился.

I'm ashamed of myself.
mnye STID-no.
Мне стыдно.

I'm shocked.
ya v SHOK-ye.
Я в шоке.

I disgust myself.
ya se-BYE pro-TI-ven.
Я себе противен.

I got so drunk, I went cruising for some tail.
ya tak na-PIL-sya, chto po-YE-khal za TYOL-ka-mi.
Я так напился, что поехал за тёлками.

I got so smashed, I woke up in the stairwell of some strange building.
ya tak bu-KHAL, chto pro-SNUL-sya v pod-YEZ-dye chu-ZHO-vo DO-ma.
Я так бухал, что проснулся в подъезде чужого дома.

I woke up in a train station outside Moscow without my pants.
ya och-NUL-sya na vok-ZAL-ye v pod-mos-KOV-ye byez svo-IKH shta-NOV.
Я очнулся на вокзале в Подмосковье без своих штанов.

I don't know how I ended up here.
ya nye ZNA-yu, kak ya syu-DA po-PAL.
Я не знаю, как я сюда попал.

I fell asleep at the table.
ya za-SNUL za sto-LOM.
Я заснул за столом.

I got thrown out of the bar.
me-NYA VI-per-li iz BAR-a.
Меня выперли из бара.

I pissed myself.
ya us-TSAL-sya.
Я усцался.

I got into a fight.
ya po-RAL-sya.
Я подрался.

I told him off and that asshole **cold-cocked me**.
*ya ye-VO po-SLAL i E-tot u-ROD **dal mnye po MOR-
dye**.*
Я его послал и этот урод **дал мне по морде**.

**A hallucination-fueled rage brought on by heavy
drinking**
BYE-la-ya go-RYACH-ka
Белая горячка
Also affectionately referred to as белочка (*BYE-loch-ka*).

Forgive me, for I have sinned.
pro-STI me-NYA, ya so-grye-SHIL.
Прости меня, я согрешил.

·····The hangover
pokh-MYE-lye
Похмелье

If you're hanging with Russians, this is gonna be a familiar
state to you. My advice? Do as the Russians do: Suck it
up and drink it off. And then promise yourself that you will
never drink that much again. At least not until the weekend.

I'm hungover.
*ya z **bo-du-NA**.*
Я с **бодуна**.

I feel like shit.
me-NYA kol-BA-sit.
Меня колбасит.

My liver hurts.
PYE-chen bo-LIT.
Печень болит.

The room is spinning.
*u me-NYA **ver-to-LYO-ti**.*
У меня **вертолёты**.
Literally, "I have helicopters."

I have dry mouth.
*u me-NYA **sush-NYAK**.*
У меня **сушняк**.

I don't remember a damn thing.
*ya **ni fi-GA** nye POM-nyu.*
Я **ни фига** не помню.

I don't remember a fucking thing.
ya ni khu-YA nye POM-nyu.
Я ни хуя не помню.

Foul breath after a night of hard drinking
pe-re-GAR
Перегар

The hair of the dog
klin KLIN-om
Клин клином

I need to drink off this hangover ASAP.
*mnye NA-do SRO-chno **o-pokh-mye-LIT-sya**.*
Мне надо срочно **опохмелиться**.

It's OK, I'll sleep it off.
*ni-che-VO, ya **o-to-SPLYUS**.*
Ничего, я **отосплюсь**.

If you can't handle a morning eye-opener, another tried-and-true Russian method of curing a hangover is drinking pickle brine, or рассол (*ra-SSOL*).

·····Alcoholics Anonymous
klub a-no-NIM-nikh al-ko-GO-li-kov
Клуб анонимных алкоголиков

Alcoholism
al-ko-go-LIZM
Алкоголизм

I gotta cut down on my drinking.
pit NA-do MYEN-she.
Пить надо меньше.

It's time to go on the wagon.
po-RA za-vya-ZAT.
Пора завязать.

I'm gonna quit tomorrow.
ya ZAV-tra BRO-shu pit.
Я завтра **брошу пить**.

To get treatment for a drinking problem
lye-CHIT-sya ot za-PO-ya
Лечиться от запоя

She's already a lost cause.
o-NA u-ZHE pro-PA-la.
Она уже **пропала**.

She's drinking her life away.
o-NA sbu-KHA-las.
Она **сбухалась**.

He drank himself to death.
on SPIL-sya.
Он **спился**.

I drank everything the fuck away.
ya pro-PIL vsyo NA khui.
Я **пропил** всё на хуй.

·····Refusing a drink
ot-KAZ
Отказ

If you're a guy, you can't refuse a drink. Sober people are not to be trusted, and if you're not drinking like everyone else, you're probably up to no good. But you can try the following feeble protests:

I'm not a drinker.
ya nye-PYU-shii.
Я непьющий.

I'm a teetotaler.
ya TRYEZ-vye-nnik.
Я трезвенник.

I've got an ulcer.
ya YAZ-vye-nnik.
Я язвенник.

I've had enough.
s me-NYA KHVA-tit.
С меня хватит.

I'm good for now.
mnye po-KA vsyo.
Мне пока всё.

I'm gonna sit this round out.
ya pas.
Я пас.

I'm too damn drunk to drink anymore.
po-mu-TI-los v moz-GU.
Помутилось в мозгу.

What, are you dissin' me?!?!
ti me-NYA nye u-va-ZHA-yesh?!?!
Ты меня не уважаешь?!?!
Expect this as the standard Russian response to someone who has tried to sit out a round.

·····Drugs
nar-KO-ti-ki
Наркотики

While drinking alcohol is still the great Russian national pastime, drugs can be scored in just about any Russian city large or small. They have become a big part of the Moscow club scene in recent years, and ecstasy-fueled raves are some of the hottest tickets in town. But get caught with dope in Russia and you will be royally screwed. So if you don't have the balls for spending a few years sharing a shower with TB-ravaged serial killers and rapists, you might want to stick to the bottle. But, hey, no one's judging here. And so...

Dope
nar-ko-TA
Наркота

I've got the goods today.
*u me-NYA se-VOD-nya **pro-DUKT**.*
У меня сегодня **продукт**.

Shit! I can't find my stash!
*blyad, nye mo-GU na-i-TI mo-YU **za-GA-shu dur-NU-yu**!*
Блядь, не могу найти мою **загашу дурную**!

Let's get high.
da-VAI po-kai-FU-yem.
Давай покайфуем.

I'm jonesing hard.
ya go-LOD-nii.
Я голодный.

How much for a bag?
*po-CHOM **ba-LLON**?*
Почём **баллон**?

I don't know why he's looking to score when he's already holding.
*mnye nye po-NYAT-no, za-CHEM on v **raz-VYED-kye** kog-DA on u-ZHE **za-TA-re-nnii**.*
Мне не понятно, зачем он **в разведке**, когда он уже **затаренный**.

I'm sick of vodka—let's get high for a change.
*mnye na-do-YE-la VOD-ka—da-VAI LU-chshe **bakh-NYOM-sya**.*
Мне надоела водка—давай лучше **бахнёмся**.

Every time he's high he gets the ganoobies.
*KAZH-dii raz, kog-DA on v TOR-bye, on **na khi-KHI pod-SA-zhi-va-yet-sya**.*
Каждый раз, когда он **в торбе**, он **на хи-хи подсаживается**.

I'm, like, totally **stoned**.
*ya, TI-pa, **po KAI-fu**.*
Я, типа, **по кайфу**.

He **gets baked** every chance he gets.
*on **LO-vit kaif** pri lyu-BOI voz-MOZH-nosti.*
Он **ловит кайф** при любой возможности.

He gets **bombed out** every fucking day.
*on **vye-RYOV-ku glo-TA-yet** KAZH-dii YO-ba-nnii dyen.*
Он **верёвку глотает** каждый ёбанный день.

Man, I hate **coming down**.
*blin, ya nye-na-VI-zhu **ot-kho-DYAK**.*
Блин, я ненавижу **отходняк**.

·····Where to score
gdye do-STAT
Где достать

Connection
go-NYETS
Гонец

Dealer
DI-ler
Дилер
In Russia, often someone from central Asia or the Caucasus, also sometimes called a Бабай (*ba-BAI*), or Басурман (*ba-sur-MAN*), among other things.

I need to find me a new **candy man**, mine doesn't know jack about dope.
*mnye NA-do na-i-TI NO-vo-vo **DOK-to-ra**, moi—dva po KU-shu.*
Мне надо найти нового **доктора**, мой—два по кушу.

I'm a total **newbie**; could you find me **a guide**?
*ya vo-ob-SHYE **pi-o-NYER**—ti MOZH-esh mnye na-i-TI **a-ri-sto-KRAT-a**?*
Я вообще **пионер**—ты можешь мне найти **аристократа**?

He didn't have any cheese, so he had to pull a **buy and fly**.
*u ne-VO NYE bi-lo BA-shlei, tak pri-SHLIOS **ot-VA-li-va-tsya ot kup-TSA**.*
У него не было башлей, так пришлось **отваливаться от купца**.

D.L. Spot
TOCH-ka
Точка

Do you know where I can score around here?
ti nye ZNA-yesh gdye tut MOZH-no VI-ru-bat?
Ты не знаешь где тут можно **вырубать**?

Their hot spot is in an old communal apartment.
*ikh **kon-TOR-a** na-KHO-dit-sya v STA-roi ko-mmu-NAL-kye.*
Их **контора** находится в старой коммуналке.

They found a new shooting gallery near the university.
*o-NI na-SHLI NO-vo-ye **BLYUD-tse** VO-zle uni-vyer-si-TYET-a.*
Они нашли новое **блюдце** возле университета.

·····Weed
trav-A
Трава

The funny thing about weed in Russia is where you'll find it growing. I once went to the Ryazan region dacha of a 60-year-old woman and saw a five-foot-tall plant, and there used to be a few smaller hemp shrubs not far from one of the embassy buildings in Ukraine. Honestly, most people don't even know what it is, and those who do know generally don't bother because the quality is such crap. If you want the good stuff, go for something from Central Asia or the Caucasus—native is total swag.

Let's smoke some...
da-VAI po-KU-rim...
Давай покурим...
Notice these words are all in the accusative.

marijuana.
ma-ri-khu-A-nu
марихуану.

pot.
a-na-shU.
анашу.

grass.
ZYE-lyen.
зелень.

bud.
pye-TRUSH-ku.
петрушку.

Mary Jane.
MAR-yu i-VA-nov-nu.
Марью Ивановну.
Also sometimes called Леди Джейн (*Lady Jane*).

cannabis.
gan-dzhu-BAS.
ганджубас.

Russian golden leaf.
A-tom
атом
Usually imported weed from places south such as Central Asia.

Hemp.
ko-no-PLYA
Конопля

Man, I'm not gonna toke that nasty-ass ditch weed.
blin, ya nye BU-du za-bi-vAt E-tu dyer-MO-vu-yu byes-pon-TOV-ku.
Блин, я не буду забивать эту дерьмовую **беспонтовку**.

This schwag ain't good, but at least it's cheap.
E-tot ko-chi-BEI khrye-NO-vii, no khot dye-SHO-vii.
Этот **кочубей** хреновый, но хоть дешёвый.

These Russian potheads only smoke dirt grass.
E-ti RU-sski-ye PLA-ne-ri KUR-yat TOL-ko KLYE-ver.
Эти русские **планеры** курят только клевер.

Aren't there any stoners in Moscow?
nye-u-ZHE-li NYET-u u-PIKH-ti-shei v mosk-VYE?
Неужели нету **упыхтышей** в Москве?

Wanna buy a dime bag?
KHO-chesh ku-PIT GA-lich-ku?
Хочешь купить **галичку**?

Where can I get some rolling papers?
gdye MOZH-no do-STAT PO-pik?
Где можно достать **попик**?

Anybody got a joint?
u ko-VO-ni-BUD YEST ko-SYAK?
У кого-нибудь есть **косяк**?

He took a hit off the joint.
on po-lu-CHIL doz-NYAK ot ko-sya-KA.
Он поучил **дозняк** от косяка.

Let's roll a fatty and spark it up.
da-VAI po-KRU-tim u-go-LYOK i po-pikh-TIM.
Давай покрутим **уголёк** и **попыхтим**.

Hey, G, let's toke this roach.
ei, pa-TSAN, da-VAI po-ku-MA-rim E-tot pye-GAS.
Эй, пацан, давай **покумарим** этот **пегас**.

Where did you put my feedbag?
gdye ti po-lo-ZHIL moi pa-KYET?
Где ты положил мой **пакет**?

Let's go buy some logs.
poi-DYOM KU-pim BYE-li-ki.
Пойдём купим **Белики**.

These are *papirosy* that can be hollowed out and filled with pot.
The full name is Беломорканал (*bye-lo-mor-ka-NAL*).

Let's kill this one.
da-VAI PYAT-ku smi-NAT.
Давай пятку сминать.

I think I have a matchbox (of pot) in the glove compartment.
po-MO-ye-mu u me-NYA yest ko-RAbL v bar-dach-KYE.
По-моему у меня есть **корабль** в бардачке.

He brought over a B, and we fired it up it together.
on pri-NYOS ko-ro-BAR i mi VMYE-stye po-du-DYE-li.
Он принёс **коробарь** и мы вместе подудели.

Another word for this is карабас (*ka-ra-BAS*).

Careful with my bong, dude.
*chu-VAK, a-kku-RAT-no s mo-IM **bul-bu-LYA-tor-om**.*
Чувак, аккуратно с моим **бульбулятором**.
Also sometimes just called a бонг.

Have you ever smoked pot through a hookah?
*ti kog-DA-ni-BUD ku-RIL tra-VU CHE-rez **ka-LYAN**?*
Ты когда-нибудь курил траву через **кальян**?

I've never seen anyone smoke from a steamroller before.
*ni-kog-DA nye VI-dyel, kak KUR-yat iz **CHIL-la**.*
Никогда не видел, как курят из **чила**.

If you shotgun weed with my girlfriend one more time, I'm gonna punch you in the mouth.
*YES-li e-SCHO raz SDYE-la-yesh **pa-ro-VOZ-ik** s mo-YEI DYE-vush-koi, to ya te-BYE dam v ROT.*
Если ещё раз сделаешь **паровозик** с моей девушкой, то я тебе дам в рот.

After smoking some ganny, he started buggin' out.
*PO-sle to-VO kak VI-ku-ril **af-GAN-ku**, on SYEL **na iz-MYE-nu**.*
После того как выкурил **афганку**, он **сел на измену**.

I blew a stick and now I've got wicked munchies.
*ya do-ku-rll dol-BAN i tye-PYER **MU-cha-yus ZHO-rom**.*
Я докурил Долбан и теперь **мучаюсь жором**.

·····Smack
BYE-lii
Белый

The hard-core addicts in Russia are generally smack-heads, so heroin has something of the reputation of being the drug of lowlife user scum. There's no dib and dab in Russia: If you use, you're likely already hooked or well on your way. But everyone chooses their poison, and if you need the Number 8, that's your business. However, keep in mind that smack has also played a huge role in Russia's

AIDS epidemic. So if you do decide to shoot up in Russia, use your own needles.

Heroin
gye-ro-IN
Героин

> I don't **shoot up H.**
> *ya nye VZHA-ri-va-yus GYE-ru.*
> Я не **вжариваюсь геру**.

> He spends all his time **mainlining**.
> *on vsyo VRYE-mya VMA-za-yet v BUL-ku.*
> Он всё время **вмазает в булку**.

> I've never seen so many **track marks** on one person before.
> *PYER-vii raz VI-zhu STOL-ko svyer-SCHEI na od-NOM chye-lo-VYE-kye.*
> Первый раз вижу столько **сверщей** на одном человеке.

> He has so many **tracks**, he looks like a train station.
> *u nye-VO STOL-ko do-ROG, chto po-KHOZH na sho-SSE.*
> У него столько **дорог**, что похож на шоссе.

> She's a junkie.
> *o-NA si-DIT na i-GLYE.*
> Она сидит на игле.

Needle
shprits
Шприц

> If you're gonna **do up some brother**, you better get a clean **spike**.
> *YES-li BU-dyesh GRI-shu gnat po VYE-nye, to LU-chshe vzyat CHI-stu-yu pya-TYEL-ku.*
> Если будешь **гришу гнать по вене**, то лучше взять чистую **пятелку**.

·····Blow

nyu-KHA-ra
Нюхара

Cocaine
ko-ka-IN
Кокаин

Do you know where I can score some snow around here?
*ti nye ZNA-yesh, gdye MOZH-no VI-ru-bat tut **snye-ZHOK**?*
Ты не знаешь, где можно вырубать тут **снежок**?

Angie is too rich for my blood.
***myel** mnye nye po kar-MA-nu.*
Мел мне не по карману.

Let's blow a line after the concert.
*da-VAI **po-nyukh-TA-rim po-NYUSH-ku** PO-sle kon-TSER-ta.*
Давай **понюхтарим понюшку** после концерта.

I saw that cokehead in the bathroom snorting flake.
*ya VI-dyel, kak E-tot **nyu-KHACH** v tua-LYE-tye **ma-ra-FYET ot-ri-VAL**.*
Я видел, как этот **нюхач** в туалете **марафет отрывал**.

·····Trippy drugs

vol-SHEB-ni-ki
Волшебники

If you're more into the club scene, ecstasy and LSD are available as well, PCP somewhat less so. While often referred to by the name on their stamp—of which there are dozens—here are the most common, general terms for LSD and XTC.

LSD
el-es-DE
ЛСД

Acid

ki-slo-TA

Кислота

> Let's drop some **Lucy** and go clubbing.
> *da-VAI pro-glo-TIM **LYU-syu** i po-klu-BIM-sya.*
> Давай проглотим **Люсю** и поклубимся.

> I scored some **blotter**.
> *ya VI-ru-bal **bu-MA-gu**.*
> Я вырубал **бумагу**.

> He's been **in transit** all night.
> *on vsyu noch **GLIU-ki LO-vit**.*
> Он всю ночь **глюки ловит**.

> That **acidhead** is always talking nonsense.
> *E-tot **gliu-ko-LOV** vseg-DA bryed bol-TA-yet.*
> Этот **глюколов** всегда бред болтает.

Ecstasy

Ek-sta-zi

Экстази

> If we're going to go clubbing tonight, I'll bring some **vitamin E.**
> *YES-li se-VOD-nya BU-dyem klu-BIT-sya, to voz-MU s so-BOI **vi-ta-MIN E**.*
> Если сегодня будем клубиться, то возьму с собой **Витамин Е.**

> How much does **Adam** usually cost in Moscow?
> *po-CHOM o-BICH-no v mosk-VYE **go-lli-VUD**?*
> Почём обычно в Москве **Голливуд**?

Rave

Рейв

> Have you ever been **to a rave**?
> *ti kog-DA-ni-BUD **bil na REI-vye**?*
> Ты когда-нибудь был **на рейве**?

PCP

Well, it's just called PCP, although sometimes you'll hear the term ангельская пыль (*AN-gyel-ska-ya pil*), or angel dust, just like back home.

▪▪▪▪▪Kiddie dope
ko-LYO-sa
Колёса

For those who can't stomach the idea of a shake down by the heat, the safest route to la-la land is through pharmaceuticals. There's an *apteka* on every corner in Russia, and it's not too hard to find a script writer if you're willing to pay. Heck, most of the time you won't even need a prescription. There are really way too many meds to name, so here are just a few of the common ones available in Russia that can get you high, low, or somewhere in between.

Ketamine
Кетамин

Bump
NAS-tya
Настя

Codeine
Кодеин

Schoolboy
ka-TYU-kha
Катюха

Morphine
MOR-fii
Морфий

White Stuff
bye-LYAN-ka
Белянка

Demerol
DYE-mik
Демик

Radedorm
RA-li-ki
Ралики

Phenobarbital
FYE-ni-ki
Феники

Noxiron
prye-zi-DYENT
Президент
Or "president" as the case may be.

Theophedrine
VOZ-dukh
Воздух
Literally, "air."

And two popular ephedrine-based poppers:

"**Jeff**"
Джэф

"**Vint**"
Винт

I'm not really into **kiddie doping**.
*mnye nye O-chen NRA-vit-sya **po ko-LYO-sam tor-CHAT***.
Мне не очень нравится **по колесам торчать**.

I think I can get that **white coat** to write me a **script**.
*po-MO-ye-mu ya smo-GU u-go-vo-RIT E-to **lye-PI-lo** mnye na-pi-SAT **chye-KUSH-ku***.
По-моему я смогу уговорить это **лепило** мне написать **чекушку**.

He spends all his time **popping pills**.
*on vsyo VRYE-mya **za-KI-di-va-yet***.
Он всё время **закидывает**.

·····Getting hooked
pod-SAD-ka
Подсадка

He just **got on** and already he's **getting hooked**.
*on nye-DAV-no NA-chal **na ZHA-lo ki-DAT** i u-ZHE **sa-DIT-sya***.
Он недавно начал **на жало кидать** и уже **садится**.

Druggie
nar-ko-MAN
Наркоман

Burnout
tor-CHOK
Торчок

> **He's permafried.**
> *on v sis-TYE-mye.*
> Он в системе.

Overdose
pye-rye-do-zi-ROV-ka
Передозировка

> **His best friend ODed** last week after a ***drug binge***.
> *ye-VO LUCH-shii drug **v ZHMUR-ki si-GRAL** na PRO-shloi nye-DYE-lye PO-sle **ma-ra-FO-na**.*
> Его лучший друг **в жмурки сыграл** на прошлой неделе после **марафона**.

They had to take him to the nuthouse after he had a freakout.
*pri-SHLOS ye-VO u-vyes-TI v **DU-roch-ku** PO-sle to-VO, kak on gu-SEI gnal.*
Пришлось его увести в **дурочку** после того, как он гусей гнал.

If she doesn't get clean, she'll end up in the boneyard.
*YES-li o-NA nye SLYE-zet, to SKO-ro ot-PRA-vit-sya v **u-CHAS-tok NO-mer tri**.*
Если она не слезет, то скоро отправится в **участок номер три**.

I don't think I can just quit cold turkey.
*ya VRYAD li smo-gU **na su-KHU-yu slyezt**.*
Я вряд ли смогу **на сухую слезть**.

I'm on the straight.
ya na ku-MA-rakh.
Я на кумарах.

CHAPTER 4

BODY RUSSIAN

TYE-LYE-SNII RU-SSKII
Телесный русский

Though fast food is becoming popular in the former Soviet Union, Russian bodies don't seem to have Supersized the way that Americans have. Most young Russians are in great shape and don't start to fatten up until 50 or so. I think the secret is that they walk ... a lot ... usually carrying ridiculously heavy bags. Most Russians—particularly women—take a lot of pride in their appearance. Even a quick trip to the *rynok* requires a dress, heels, and full makeup. It's pretty rare to catch a young Russian woman in public wearing sweats and sneakers. They like to look good for any occasion, and a big part of that is keeping their bodies tight and supple. Ain't nothing wrong with that!

·····Body
TYE-lo
Тело

He's got a nice six pack.
*u nye-VO kho-RO-shii **pryess**.*
У него хороший **пресс**.

♈ BLOODY MARY À LA RUSSE

The quickest way to cure a hangover is with a Bloody Mary. And this version with cucumber and pickles is straight from the soul of Russia. Assuming you can peel yourself off the bathroom floor and get to the kitchen, this will do the trick.

GET THESE:

4 slices fresh cucumber
2 ounces vodka
5 ounces tomato juice
$\frac{1}{2}$ ounce lemon juice
1 to 2 dashes Tabasco, to taste
$\frac{1}{4}$ teaspoon mustard
$\frac{1}{4}$ teaspoon horseradish
salt and pepper, to taste
pickle, for garnish

DO THIS:

Place the fresh cucumber in a glass and mash with a muddler. Add the vodka, tomato juice, lemon juice, Tabasco, mustard, horseradish, and salt and pepper. Thoroughly mix all the ingredients, then add ice. Garnish with a pickle. Take 2 pain relievers and sip slowly.

He's got a big **belly**.
*u nye-VO bol-SHO-ye **PU-zo***.
У него большое **пузо**.

She has **amazing legs**.
*u nye-YO **o-bal-DYE-nni-ye NO-zhki***.
У неё **обалденные ножки**.

He's got a **cute butt**.
*u nye-VO **sim-pa-TICH-na-ya PO-pa***.
У него **симпатичная попа**.

She's got a **great chest**.
*u nye-YO **KLASS-na-ya grud***.
У неё **классная грудь**.

You've got **beautiful eyes**.
*u te-BYA **kra-SI-vi-ye gla-ZI-sche***.
У тебя **красивые глазищи**.

She's got a pretty nice kisser.
*u nye-YO nye-plo-KHA-ya **mor-DASH-ka**.*
У неё неплохая **мордашка**.

He has a stupid mug.
*u nye-VO tu-PA-ya **MOR-da**.*
У него тупая **морда**.

She has big teeth like a beaver.
*o-NA **zu-BA-sta-ya** kak bo-BYOR.*
Она **зубастая** как бобёр.

He's bearded like a lumberjack.
*on **bo-ro-DA-tii** kak dro-vo-SYEK.*
Он **бородатый** как дровосек.

He's got a double chin.
*u nye-VO **vto-ROI pod-bo-RO-dok**.*
У него **второй подбородок**.

She's got nasty saddlebags.
*u nye-YO pro-TIV-ni-ye **U-shi na BYO-drakh**.*
У неё противные **уши на бёдрах**.

He has a big schnozz.
*u nye-VO **nos kartOshkoi**.*
У него **нос картошкой**.

Her ass is so wide it needs its own zip code.
*ye-YO **ZHO-pa** na-STOL-ko shi-ro-KA, chto TRYE-bu-yet svo-ye-VO IN-dyek-sa.*
Её **жопа** настолько широка, что требует своего индекса.

Sexy
SYE-ksi
Секси

I don't know what it is about the Slavs, but overall they are a damn fine-looking people. High cheekbones, slightly Asian eyes, and those exotic rolled *r*'s—all together, they make for one sexy package.

He's in really good shape.
*on v O-chen kho-RO-shei **FOR-mye**.*
Он в очень хорошей **форме**.

She's really built.
o-NA O-chen STROI-na-ya.
Она очень **стройная**.

He's such a stud.
on zhe-rye-BYETS.
Он **жеребец**.

You've got a fuckin' hot bod!
u te-BYA o-khu-YE-nna-ya fi-GU-ra!
У тебя **охуенная фигура!**

He's a hottie (male).
on kra-SAV-chik.
Он **красавчик**.

That hottie (female) is gonna be with me tonight.
E-ta chik-SA BU-dyet so MNOI se-VOD-nya.
Эта **чикса** будет со мной сегодня.
From the English word "chick" but with more of a sexy feel.

She's real purty.
o-NA smaz-LI-vyen-ka-ya.
Она **смазливенькая**.

Damn, she's a nice piece of ass!
blin, o-NA ta-KA-ya pro-PYEZ-do-loch!
Блин, она такая **пропездолоч!**

He ain't bad!
da on ni-che-VO!
Да он **ничего!**

She is fucking hot!
o-NA ye-BLI-va-ya!
Она **ебливая!**

Damn, you…!
blin, nu ti i…!
Блин, ну ты и…!

> **fine**
> *shi-KAR-nii/shi-KAR-na-ya*
> шикарный/шикарная

smokin'
po-TRYAS-nii/po-TRYAS-na-ya
потрясный/потрясная

real cute
kho-RO-shen-kii/kho-RO-shen-ka-ya
хорошенький/хорошенькая

gorgeous
o-fi-GYE-nnii/o-fi-GYE-nna-ya
офигенный/офигенная

sexy
syeks-a-PIL-nii/syeks-a-PIL-na-ya
сексапильный/сексапильная

•••••Ugly
u-ROD-li-vii
Уродливый

Because we can't all be born beautiful.

He needs to go on a diet.
ye-MU po-RA syest na di-YE-tu.
Ему пора **сесть на диету**.

She's a fucking skeleton.
o-NA khu-do-YO-bi-na.
Она **худоёбина**.

She's anorexic.
o-NA stra-DA-yet a-no-ryek-SI-ye.
Она страдает **анорексией**.

Her fingers are all yellow from bulimia.
ye-YO PAL-tsi vsye zhel-TYE-yut ot bu-LI-mii.
Ёе пальцы все желтеют от **булимии**.

He's as hunchbacked as a camel.
on gor-BA-tii kak vyer-BLYUD.
Он **горбатый** как верблюд.

She's a four-eyes.
o-NA och-KAS-ta-ya.
Она **очкастая**.

He's as bug-eyed as a dragonfly.
u nye-VO gla-ZA na-VI-kat, kak u strye-koz-I.
У него **глаза навыкат**, как у стрекозы.

She's a bleached blonde.
o-NA KRA-she-nna-ya blon-DIN-ka.
Она **крашенная блондинка**.

She is butt ugly.
o-NA KLU-sha.
Она **клуша**.

She's a hairy mess.
o-NA do bye-zo-BRA-zi-ya vo-lo-SA-ta-ya.
Она до безобразия **волосатая**.

He's a fat ass.
on zho-PA-stii.
Он **жопастый**.

Damn, you…!
blin, nu ti i…!
Блин, ну ты и…!

> **hideous**
> *bye-zo-BRAZ-nii/bye-zo-BRAZ-na-ya*
> безобразный/безобразная
>
> **nasty**
> *PA-kost-nii/PA-kost-na-ya*
> пакостный/пакостная
>
> **gross**
> *pro-TIV-nii/pro-TIV-na-ya*
> противный/противная
>
> **disgusting**
> *ot-vra-TI-tyel-nii/ot-vra-TI-tyel-na-ya*
> отвратительный/отвратительная
>
> **fugly**
> *u-YO-bisch-nii/u-YO-bisch-na-ya*
> уёбищный/уёбищная

·····Illness

bo-LYEZN
Болезнь

Another, more cynical, explanation for those slender Russian bods is that many Russians are prone to illness. It could be the harsh climate, exposure to radiation and pollution, unbalanced nutrition, limited access to competent health care, or all the drinking and smoking most people seem to do, but Russians seem to get sick. A lot.

What's wrong with you?
CHTO s to-BOI?
Что с тобой?

I feel really shitty.
*ya **khrye-NO-vo** se-BYA CHUST-vu-yu.*
Я **хреново** себя чувствую.

I'd be better off dead.
zhi-VI-ye za-VI-du-yut MYORT-vim.
Живые завидуют мёртвым.
Literally, "the living envy the dead."

You look like crap.
ti khye-RO-vo VI-glya-dish.
Ты херово выглядишь.

My head is pounding.
bash-KA bo-LIT.
Башка болит.

I have high blood pressure.
*u me-NYA vi-SO-ko-ye **da-VLYE-ni-ye**.*
У меня высокое **давление**.
This is a farily common complaint among old and young alike.

I've been down in the dumps all week.
*u me-NYA TSE-lu-yu nye-DYE-liu **dye-pryess-NYAK**.*
У меня целую неделю **депрессняк**.

I have angina.
*u me-NYA **an-GI-na**.*
У меня **ангина**.
I don't think I had ever heard of angina until I went to Russia, but this is something that Russians seem to complain about a lot.

It usually just seems to be something along the lines of a sore throat.

Do you have anything for heartburn?
*u te-BYA YEST chto-ni-BUD ot **iz-ZHO-gi**?*
У тебя есть что-нибудь от **изжоги**?

I have a fever.
*u me-NYA **tyem-pye-ra-TU-ra**.*
У меня **температура**.

I'm nauseous.
me-NYA tosh-NIT.
Меня тошнит.

I've got the shakes.
me-NYA TRU-sit.
Меня трусит.

I can't think straight.
u me-NYA bash-KA nye VA-rit.
У меня башка не варит.

Do you need a prescription for these antibiotics?
*NU-zhen li **rye-TSEPT** dlya E-tikh an-ti-bi-O-ti-kov?*
Нужен ли **рецепт** для этих антибиотиков?
In Russia, the answer more often than not is no.

·····Sleep
son
Сон

If you ask me, the best thing to do for an illness is to sleep it off. Note that the word сон in Russian means both "sleep" and the kind of dream that you have when sleeping. There is also another word for dream in Russian—мечта (*myech-TA*)—but that's more like the kind of dream that Martin Luther King Jr. had.

I'm tired as a dog.
ya u-STAL kak so-BA-ka.
Я устал как собака.

IF YOU SIT ON CONCRETE, YOUR OVARIES WILL FREEZE)))

YES-LI PO-SI-DISH NA BE-TO-NYE, TO YA-ICH-NI-KI OT-MYOR-ZNUT

ЕСЛИ ПОСИДИШЬ НА БЕТОНЕ, ТО ЯИЧНИКИ ОТМЁРЗНУТ

If you ask Russians why they're sick, nine times out of ten they'll blame the weather or a problem involving atmospheric pressure or the fact that they sat on concrete under a clear sky while not wearing a hat. Russians have some medical beliefs that will seem straight up bizarre to Westerners. But don't even try to argue with them about health. No matter how outlandish their claims, they will be convinced that they are right, and it will be a waste of time trying to change their minds. Here are some of the weird reasons why Russians think they get sick and the weirder cures they use to heal themselves.

A lot of people feel ill today because of the **atmospheric pressure**.
*MHO-gi-ye sye-VOD-nya bo-LE-yut iz-za **da-VLYE-ni-ya v at-mo-SFYER-ye**.*
Многие сегодня болеют из-за **давления в атмосфере**.

If you **sit in the draft**, you'll catch a cold.
*YES-li **po-si-DISH v skvoz-nya-KYE**, to pro-STU-dish-sya.*
Если **посидишь в сквозняке**, то простудишься.

I had a drink with ice, and now my throat hurts.
***ya VI-pil na-PI-tok so I-DOM** i tye-PYER u me-NYA GOR-lo bo-LIT.*
Я выпил напиток со льдом и теперь у меня горло болит.

He got sick because he wasn't wearing a hat.
on za-bo-LYEL, po-to-MU chto SHAP-ku nye no-SIL.
Он заболел, потому что шапку не носил.

I'm worn out.
ya u-STAV-shii.
Я уставший.

I'm sleepy.
*mnye KHO-chet-sya **spat**.*
Мне хочется **спать**.

Someone must have **given me the evil eye**, because I've been getting sick a lot lately.
KTO-to na-VYER-no **me-NYA SGLA-zil**, *po-to-MU chto v po-SLYED-nye-ye VRYE-mya ya CHAS-to bo-LYE-yu.*
Кто-то наверное **меня сглазил**, потому что в последнее время я часто болею.

One hundred grams of vodka with pepper **will cure** anything.
sto GRAM VOD-ki s PYER-tsem **VI-lye-chat** *te-BYA ot vsye-VO.*
Сто грамм водки с перцем **вылечат** тебя от всего.

After I got the flu, my granny healed me with **mustard plasters**.
PO-sle to-VO, kak za-bo-LYEL GRI-ppom, mo-YA BAB-ka VI-lye-chi-la me-NYA **gor-CHICH-ni-ka-mi**.
После того как заболел гриппом, моя бабка вылечила меня **горчичниками**.

Mustard plasters are still a pretty popular way to treat respiratory illnesses in Russia.

I cured my stuffy nose by **inhaling potato vapors**.
ya svoi NAS-mork VI-lye-chil CHE-ryez **vdi-KHA-ni-ye kar-TO-fyel-no-vo PA-ra**.
Я свой насморк вылечил через **вдыхание картофельного пара**.

I always treat a cold with **fire cupping**.
ya vseg-DA LYE-chu pro-STU-du **BAN-ka-mi**.
Я всегда лечу простуду **банками**.

If you've never heard of fire cupping, it basically involves lighting a match in little glass jars to create suction and then sticking them onto a sick person's back.

My aunt cured her cancer with **special herbal tea**.
mo-YA TYO-tya iz-lye-CHI-la se-BYA ot RA-ka **spye-tsi-AL-ni-mi cha-YA-mi na TRAV-kakh**.
Моя тётя излечила себя от рака **специальными чаями на травках**.

I want to **take a nap**.
kho-CHU **po-drye-MAT**.
Хочу **подремать**.

I'm on bed rest.
ya v SPAL-nom rye-ZHI-mye.
Я в спальном режиме.

It's time for me to go beddy-bye.
*mnye po-RA **SPAT-ki**.*
Мне пора **спатки**.

I just feel like lying around in bed today.
*sye-VOD-nya KHO-chet-sya PRO-sto **po-va-LYAT-sya
v po-STYE-li**.*
Сегодня хочется просто **поваляться в постели**.

I overslept today.
*ya sye-VOD-nya **pro-SPAL**.*
Я сегодня **проспал**.

**I'm gonna read a few more pages and then get
some shut-eye.**
*ya pro-CHTU ye-SCHO PA-ru stra-NITS, a po-TOM **MA-
ssu po-da-VLYU**.*
Я прочту ещё пару страниц, а потом **массу
подавлю**.

I usually watch some telly before bed.
PYE-red snom ya o-BICH-no smo-TRYU TYE-lik.
Перед сном я обычно смотрю телик.

He snores like a pig.
on khra-PIT kak svi-NYA.
Он храпит как свинья.

I suffer from insomnia.
*ya stra-DA-yu ot **byes-SON-ni-tsi**.*
Я страдаю от **бессонницы**.

·····The Russian bathhouse
RU-sska-ya BA-nya
Русская баня

One of things I love most about Russia is the *banya*. Hey,
it's fun to hang out naked with your friends. And if you
believe the Russians, steamin' it up in the bathhouse is one
of the keys to good health, and being beaten with birch
branches is a surefire way to release all of those toxins
you've built up swilling vodka. Now who am I to argue with
that?

Let's go for a steam!
da-VAI po-PA-rim-sya!
Давай попаримся!

Have a good steam!
s LYO-gkim PA-rom!
С лёгким паром!

This is what you say to someone on his way to the *banya*. If you've ever spent New Year's in Russia, you probably know this phrase from the classic Soviet film of the same name.

Where can I buy a felt *banya* hat around here?
*gdye tut MOZH-no ku-PIT **CHAP-ku**?*
Где тут можно купить **чапку**?

Let's leave our clothes in the changing area.
*da-VAI o-DYEZH-du o-STA-vim v **pryed-BA-nni-kye**.*
Давай одежду оставим в **предбаннике**.

Let's hit the steam room.
*poi-DYOM v **pa-RIL-ku**.*
Пойдём в **парилку**.

Hey, Vasya, could you beat me with that branch a little more?
*eh, VA-sya, ti MO-zhesh me-NYA ye-SCHO chut **po-PA-rit VYE-nich-kom**?*
Эй, Вася, ты можешь меня ещё чуть **попарить веничком**?

Vasya is a common Russian guy's name, but it is also sometimes used with random people in a sort of cheeky way.

Now that we've steamed up, let's go jump in the snow!

tye-PYER, kak kho-ro-SHO po-PA-ri-lis, poi-DYOM po-PRI-ga-yem v snyeg!

Теперь, как хорошо попарились, пойдём попрыгаем в снег!

Steamin' it up is usually followed by a cold shower, a jump in a cold lake, or, in wintertime, a naked roll in the snow. It's all about the hot and cold contrasts.

I prefer white *banyas*.

*ya pryed-po-chi-TA-yu **BA-nyu po-BYEL-omu**.*

Я предпочитаю **баню по-белому**.

There are two basic types of *banya*: white *banya* (по-белому) and black *banya* (по-чёрному). White *banyas* are usually a bit better as the smoke is vented through pipes. In black *banyas*, the smoke just goes through a hole in the ceiling.

He drank too much vodka and steamed himself to death.

on pye-rye-BRAL VOD-ku i za-PA-ril-sya.

Он перебрал водки и запарился.

Which does happen apparently.

·····The crapper
sor-TIR
Сортир

Public restrooms are in short supply in Russia, and the ones that do exist are pretty rank. The most unfortunate type consists of a hole in the ground covered up by some rotting pieces of wood and covered with piss, shit, and those little squares of newspaper that people use for toilet paper. The better ones actually have a toilet, even if it just some metal-porcelain contraption that you squat over. So if you need to answer nature's call while out and about in Russia, your best bet is probably to find a Mickey D's where you can sit your ass down in relative luxury.

Yesterday I spent all day sitting on the potty.

ya vchye-RA TSE-lii dyen si-DYEL na gor-SHKYE.

Я вчера целый день сидел на горшке.

I gotta go to the toilet.
*mnye NA-do **v uni-TAZ**.*
Мне надо **в унитаз**.

Where's the nearest crapper?
*gdye SA-mii bli-ZHAI-ishii **sor-TIR**?*
Где самый ближайший **сортир**?

Let's go to the john.
*poi-DYOM v **u-BOR-nu-yu**.*
Пойдём в **уборную**.

That shithole is really nasty.
*E-ta **pa-RA-sha** SIL-no pro-TIV-na-ya.*
Эта **параша** сильно противная.
This is usually the word used for the holes in the ground that prisoners crap in.

·····Urine
mo-CHA
Моча

If you're a woman, the upside to the prevalence of the Turkish toilet in Russia is that after a few months of squatting over the piss hole, you'll have thighs you can crack coconuts with.

When I drink beer, I have to urinate every five minutes.
*kog-DA ya PI-vo pyu, mnye NA-do **mo-CHIT-sya** KAZH-di-ye pyat mi-NUT.*
Когда я пиво пью, мне надо **мочиться** каждые пять минут.

I want to go pee-pee.
ya kho-CHU pi PI.
Я хочу пи пи.

I gotta pee bad.
*mnye SROCH-no NA-do **po-PI-sat**.*
Мне срочно надо **пописать**.
Watch your stress here. To pee is *PI-sat*. With the accent on the second syllable (*pi-SAT*), it just means "to write."

I gotta go **number one.**
*mnye NA-do **po DYET-sko-mu/po MA-lyen-ko-ty**.*
Мне надо по **детскому/по маленькому**.

I think I need **to tinkle.**
*po-MO-ye-ti mnye NA-do **BRIZ-nut**.*
По-моему мне надо **брызнуть**.

I really **gotta piss.**
*mnye O-chen NA-do **pos-SAT**.*
Мне очень надо **поссать**.

I laughed so hard I **wet myself.**
*ya tak sme-YAL-sya, chto **o-bos-SAL-sya**.*
Я так смеялся, что **обоссался**.

Even in school he was still a **bedwetter.**
*DA-zhe v SHKOL-ye on ye-SCHO bil **ssi-ku-NOM**.*
Даже в школе он ещё был **ссыкуном**.

·····Shit
gav-NO
Гавно

I think the most promising sign of Russia's economic upturn is the availability of white toilet paper. Don't get me wrong, you still likely won't find anything as squeezable as Charmin, but it sure beats the hell out of that stretchy brown crepe paper that used to pass for toilet paper back in the old days. Although keep in mind that if you think you'll need to wipe your ass out in public, you might want to carry some with you, as most public restrooms lack this basic supply.

I wanna **poop.**
*kho-CHU **po-KA-kat**.*
Хочу **покакать**.

Where can I **take a dump?**
*gdye tut MOZH-no **po-SRAT**?*
Где тут можно **посрать**?

I gotta go **number two.**
*mnye NA-do **po VZRO-slo-mu/po bol-SHO-mu**.*
Мне надо **по взрослому/по большому**.

There's some doodie on the floor.
na po-LU yest chut ka-KA-shek.
На полу есть чуть **какашек**.

That shit really stinks.
E-to gov-NO FU kak vo-NYA-yet.
Это **говно** фу как воняет.

It smells like crap here.
tut PAKH-nyet dyer-MOM.
Тут пахнет **дерьмом**.

I have nasty diarrhea.
u me-NYA SIL-nii po-NOS.
У меня сильный **понос**.

After I ate at that shitty restaurant, I got the runs.
PO-sle to-VO, kak po-KU-shal v E-tom khrye-NO-vom res-to-RA-nye, u me-NYA po-ya-VI-las DRIS-nya.
После того, как покушал в этом хреновом ресторане, у меня появилась **дрисня**.

I'm feeling a bit constipated.
u me-NYA chut za-POR.
У меня чуть **запор**.

·····Farting
PU-kan-i-ye
Пукание

Farting is no more publicly acceptable in Russia than it is in the U.S. Fortunately, however, there is usually some stinking drunkard around that you can blame it on.

I'm a little gassy.
u me-NYA GA-zi-ki.
У меня **газики**.

He's a nasty farter.
on pro-TIV-nii VI-pyer-dish.
Он противный **выпердыш**.

He let out a loud fart.
on GROM-ko PUK-nul.
Он громко **пукнул**.

Hey, who cut the cheese?
*eh, kto **PYORD-nul**?*
Эй, кто **пёрднул**?

That one was silent but deadly.
*E-to bil **vo-NYU-chii bzdyekh**.*
Это был **вонючий бздех**.

•••••Puke
blye-VO-ti-na
Блевотина

Puking sucks. Unfortunately, it is often a part of international travel since undercooked meat and heavy drinking can take its toll on the gut pretty quickly.

I gotta hurl.
*mnye NA-do **po-ri-GAT**.*
Мне надо **порыгать**.
Рыгать can also mean to blelch.

I'm gonna toss chunk.
mnye NA-do po-stru-GAT.
Мне надо постругать.

Every time I see him I wanna barf.
*KAZH-dii raz, kog-DA ya ye-VO VI-zhu, KHO-chet-sya **blye-VAT**.*
Каждый раз, когда я его вижу, хочется **блевать**.

That moonshine made me loose my lunch.
ya po-ka-ZAL za-KUS-ku ot E-to-vo sa-mo-GO-na.
Я показал закуску от этого самогона.

•••••Other bodily excretions
dru-GI-ye tye-LYES-ni-ye vi-dye-LYE-ni-ya
Другие телесные выделения

One of the things that has always disgusted me about the provinces is the number of old men perfectly willing to use the old farmer's blow while hobbling along the street.

I mean, I guess it's better than using your hand, but still, that's pretty nasty.

Spit
SLYU-ni
Слюни

Snot
SOP-li
Сопли

Yuck! Don't **blow your nose** on your hand!
*fuuu! Ne NA-do **smor-KAT-sya** v RU-ku!*
Фууу! Не надо **сморкаться** в руку!

Stop picking your nose!
KHVA-tit ko-vi-RYAT v no-SU!
Хватит ковырять в носу!

Gross! You got **boogers** hanging out of your nose!
*FU pro-TIV-no! u te-BYA iz NOs-a tor-CHAT **ko-ZYAV-ki**!*
Фу противно! У тебя из носа торчат **козявки**!

Menstruation
myen-stru-A-tsi-ya
Менструация

I've got my **period**.
*u me-NYA **MYE-syach-ni-ye**.*
У меня **месячные**.

It's her time of the month.
u nye-YO kri-TI-ches-ki-ye dni.
У неё критические дни.

I'm on **the rag**.
*u me-NYA **bo-LO-to**.*
У меня **болото**.

Where can I buy some **pads**?
*gdye MOZH-no ku-PIT **pro-KLAD-ki**?*
Где можно купить **прокладки**?

Do you have an extra tampon?
YEST u te-BYA LISH-nii tam-PON?
Есть у тебя лишний тампон?

CHAPTER 5

HORNY RUSSIAN

VOZ-BUZH-DYO-NII RU-SSKII
Возбуждённый русский

There used to be a saying that there was no sex in the Soviet Union. Well, Russians have come a long way since then and, like many European cultures, now make Americans look like the puritanical prudes who founded our country.

·····Screwing
TRA-kha-nie
Траханье

Let's...
da-VAI...
Давай...

do it.
SDYE-la-yem E-to.
сделаем это.
With emphasis on the *eto*.

have sex.
po-za-ni-MA-yem-sya SYEKS-som.
позанимаемся сексом.

make love.
po-za-ni-MA-yem-sya liu-BO-viu.
позанимаемся любовью.

🍸 BUMPING FUZZY RUSSIANS

If you want to bump fuzzies after dinner, then you should begin the meal with a brace of Fuzzy Russians. That'll set the mood.

GET THESE:
1 ounce vodka
1 ounce peach schnapps
4 ounces freshly squeezed orange juice

DO THIS:
Put all the ingredients into a cocktail shaker with ice. Shake and strain into a rocks glass with fresh ice. Sip and get ready to take it to the next level.

screw.
po-TRA-kha-yem-sya.
потрахаемся.

fuck.
po-ye-BYOM-sya.
поебёмся.

bang.
po-FAK-a-yem-sya.
пофакаемся.
From the English verb "to fuck."

get sweaty.
BA-nya po-PA-rit-sa.
баня попариться.

We screwed all night.
mi TRA-kha-lis vsyu noch.
Мы трахались всю ночь.

Fuck me!
ye-BI me-NYA!
Еби меня!

I usually have sex about three times a week.
ya o-BICH-no za-ni-MA-yus SEKS-om RA-za tri v nye-DYE-lyu.
Я обычно занимаюсь сексом раза три в неделю.

I really need a good screw.
mnye O-chen NA-do kho-RO-shu-yu SHVOR-ku.
Мне очень надо хорошую шворку.

From the moment we met, I've wanted to nail her.
*c mo-MYEN-ta zna-KOM-stva, ya tak kho-CHU yei **PAL-ku KI-nut**.*
С момента знакомства, я так хочу ей **палку кинуть**.

After dinner we bumped fuzzies.
*PO-sle U-zhi-na mi **i-GRA-li na vo-lo-SYAN-kye**.*
После ужина мы **играли на волосянке**.

He gave me a really good lay.
*on me-NYA **na-YA-ri-val na vo-lo-SYAN-kye**.*
Он меня **наяривал на волосянке**.

I'm really turned on by chicks wearing ass floss.
*me-NYA tak **voz-buzh-DA-yut** DYEV-ki **v zho-po-RYE-zakh**.*
Меня так **возбуждают** девки в **жопорезах**.

Let's have a quickie.
da-VAI po BIS-tro-mu.
Давай по быстрому.

More! More!
ye-SCHO! ye-SCHO!
Ещё! Ещё!

Oh, that tickles!
oy, E-to sche-KOT-no!
Ой, это щекотно!

Ouch! Watch out for my pubes!
oy! Ak-ku-RAT-no s vo-lo-SYAN-koi!
Ой! Аккуратно s волосянкой!

·····Virginity
DYEV-stvyen-nost
Девственность

If you're one of those guys who's come to Russia thinking you'll find some hot young virgin to marry, you will probably be disappointed. While she may be hot and she may be young, chances are if she tells you she's a virgin, she is either lying or under 14.

Please be gentle, I'm a...
NYEZH-no, po-ZHA-lui-sta, ya...
Нежно, пожалуйста, я...

> **virgin (male).**
> *DYEV-stvyen-nik.*
> девственник.

> **virgin (female).**
> *DYEV-stvyen-ni-tsa.*
> девственница.

I can't believe she told you that she's an iron box.
*mnye nye VYER-i-tsa, chto o-NA te-BYE ska-ZA-la, chto **TSEL-ka**.*
Мне не верится, что она тебе сказала, что **целка**.

SUCK MY...)))

OT-SO-SI MOI...
ОТСОСИ МОЙ...

All of these requests—with the exception of "spank"—will be followed by a noun in the accusative case.

Lick my
b-LI-zi-vai moi/mo-YU...
Облизывай мой/мою

Kiss my
po-tse-LUI moi/mo-YU
Поцелуй мой/мою

Smooch my
...CHMO-kai-sya moi/ mo-YU
Чмокайся мой/мою

Tickle my
...po-sche-ko-CHI moi/ mo-YU...
Пощекочи мой/мою

Touch my
...TRO-gai moi/mo-YU...
Трогай мой/мою

Feel my
...po-SHU-pai moi/mo-YU...
Пощупай мой/мою

Feel up my
...LA-pai moi/mo-YU...
Лапай мой/мою

Grope my
...MA-tsai moi/mo-YU...
Мацай мой/мою

Bite my
y-ku-SI moi/mo-YU...
Укуси мой/мою

Spank my
...po-KHLO-pai mnye po...
Похлопай мне по
(plus dative)

Massage my
...mas-sa-ZHI-rui moi/ mo-YU...
Массажируй мой/ мою

Friday night I'm gonna make her a woman.
v PYAT-ni-tsu VYE-che-rom, ya ye-YO o-BA-bliu.
В пятницу вечером, я **её обаблю**.

I popped her cherry and now she won't stop calling me.
ya yei TSEL-ku pro-lo-MAL i o-NA tye-PYER ne pye-rye-sta-YOT mnye zvo-NIT.
Я **ей целку проломал** и она теперь не перестаёт мне звонить.

·····Ass
ZHO-pa
Жопа

Cuz there's nothing like a big ol' butt.

Stick it in my…
vstav mnye v…
Вставь мне в…

Let's do it in the…
da-VAI v…
Давай в…
The following are all in the accusative.

butt.
PO-pu.
попу.

booty.
an-ti-FEIS.
антифейс.
Get it? Anti-face.

backdoor.
och-KO.
очко.

bum.
GUZ-no.
гузно.

heinie.
PO-poch-ku.
попочку.

bung hole.
vyer-ZO-khu.
верзоху.

buttapest.
po-pyen-GA-gyen.
попенгаген.
A play on the word for "butt" (*popa*) and the city name
Copenhagen.

bumper.
BAM-per.
бампер.

buns.
ba-TO-ni.
батоны.

bottom.
ZAD-ni-tsu.
задницу.

•••••Dick
khui
Хуй

Most Russian men are uncut, the way nature made them.
And like men all around the world, they have a large range
of pet names for their little friend in their pants.

Suck my...
ot-so-SI moi...
Отсоси мой...

Jerk off my...
dro-CHI moi...
Дрочи мой...
Also, all in the accusative.

penis.
PYE-nis.
пенис.

member.
chlyen.
член.

cock.
khryen.
хрен.

johnson.
kher.
хер.

rod.
PAL-ku.
палку.

pee pee (the body part, not the liquid that comes out of it).
PIS-ku.
письку.
This can refer to both male and female genitalia.

sausage.
kol-BA-si-nu.
колбасину.

weiner.
sar-DYEL-ku.
сардельку.

teeny wienie.
sche-ko-TUN.
щекотун.

little prick.
khu-ISH-ko.
хуишко.

bone.
KOS-toch-ku.
косточку.

I've never blown an uncut dick before!
ya ni-kog-DA nye ot-so-SA-la nye-ob-RYE-zan-nii khui!
Я никогда не отсосала необрезанный хуй!

I'm gonna put my gag in her mouth.
ya VSTA-vlyu moi klyap v ye-YO rot.
Я вставлю мой **кляп** в её рот.

Man, did it hurt when she bit my piece.
blin, kak BI-lo BOL-no kog-DA o-NA u-ku-SI-la moi shish.
Блин, как было больно когда она укусила мой **шиш**.

BLOW JOBS)))

MI-NYE-TI
МИНЕТЫ

I could really use a **blow job**.
mnye bi NA-do mi-NYET.
Мне бы надо **минет**.

Blow me!
ot-so-SI u me-NYA!
Отсоси у меня!

Gimme some head!
SDYE-lai mnye ot-SOS!
Сделай мне отсос!

Come on, **smoke my pipe**.
da-VAI ku-RI mo-YU TRUB-ku.
Давай **кури мою трубку**.

She's really a pro at playing the skin flute.
o-NA MAS-ter po i-GRYE na KO-zha-noi FLEIT-ye.
Она мастер по игре на кожаной флейте.

Wanna suck my lollipop?
khoch po-so-SAT mo-YU kon-FYET-ku?
Хочь пососать мою конфектку?

I wanna cum in your mouth.
ya kho-CHU KON-chit v rot.
Я хочу кончить в рот.

Here comes my little baldy!
*vot i-DYOT moi **MA-lyen-kii plyesh**!*
Вот идёт мой **маленький плешь**!

Have you ever seen a schlong this big?
*ti kog-DA-ni-BUD VI-dye-la ta-KOI bol-SHOI **SHMAI-ser**?*
Ты когда-нибудь видела такой большой **шмайсер**?

Hope you got a fire, 'cause I brought the skewer.
*na-DYE-yus, chto u te-BYA yest o-GON, po-to-MU chto ya pri-NYOS **SHAM-pur**.*
Надеюсь, что у тебя есть огонь, потому что я принёс **шампур**.

Open your mouth and get ready for my
thermometer.
*ot-KROI rot i go-TOV-sya k mo-ye-MU **GRA-dus-ni-ku***.
Открой рот и готовься к моему **градуснику**.

•••••Balls
YAI-tsa
Яйца

She fucked me so hard my **nuts** hurt.
*o-NA tak SIL-no me-NYA ye-BLA, chto bo-LYE-li mo-I
YO-bal-di*.
Она так сильно меня ебла, что болели мои
ёбалды.

Do my **marbles** seem too big to you?
*mo-I **ko-lo-KOL-chi-ki** te-BYE nye KA-zhut-sa SLISH-
kom bol-SHI-ye?*
Мои **колокольчики** тебе не кажутся слишком
большие?

I pissed her off, and she kicked me in the **nads**.
*ya ye-YO ra-zo-ZLIL, i o-NA da-LA mnye v **ak-ku-mu-
LYA-to-ri***.
Я её разозлил, и она дала мне в **аккумуляторы**.

I love when she licks my **junk**.
*ya liu-BLYU kog-DA o-NA ob-LI-zi-va-yet moi **pri-BOR***.
Я люблю когда она облизывает мой **прибор**.

•••••Tits
SI-ski
Сиськи

If you're a guy, I suppose one of the perks of Russia is the
number of tits you will likely see. There seems to be no
short supply of young braless women in skimpy shirts who
turn all of Russia into one big wet T-shirt contest with the
first rains of spring.

Squeeze my...
TIS-kai mnye...
Тискай мне...

Pinch my…
po-shi-PAI mnye…
Пощипай мне…

> **breasts.**
> *GRU-di.*
> груди.

> **boobs.**
> *DO-ki.*
> доки.

> **tatas.**
> *SAI-zi.*
> сайзы.

> **tits.**
> *SI-ski.*
> сиськи.

> **titties.**
> *TIT-ki.*
> титьки.

> **nipples.**
> *sos-KI.*
> соски.

I prefer tiny titties.
*ya pryed-po-chi-TA-yu ma-LYU-syen-ki-ye **TIT-ki**.*
Я предпочитаю малюсенькие **титьки**.

When I took off her bra, the twins just about hit me in the face.
*kog-DA ya snyal ye-YO LIF-chik, ye-YO **bu-fe-rA** chut ne u-DA-ri-li mnye v li-TSO.*
Когда я снял её лифчик, её **буфера** чуть не ударили мне в лицо.

She wears the biggest boulder holder I've ever seen.
*o-NA NO-sit SA-mye bol-SHI-ye **SHA-poch-ki bliz-nyet-SOV**, ko-TOR-i-ye ya kog-DA-ni-BUD VI-dyel.*
Она носит самые большие **шапочки близнецов**, которые я когда-нибудь видел.

Man, she has some nasty flapjacks.
*blin, u nye-YO pro-TIV-ni-ye **U-shi shpa-ni-YEl-ya**.*
Блин, у неё противные **уши спаниеля**.

•••••Pussy
piz-DA
Пизда

Lick my...
po-li-ZHI mnye...
Полижи мне...

Shave my...
po-BRYEi mnye
Побрей мне...
The following are all in the accusative.

vagina.
vla-GA-li-sche.
влагалище.

muff.
MAN-du.
манду.

cunt.
schyel.
щель.

hole.
DIR-ku.
дырку.

beaver.
loch-MA-tii seif.
лохматый сейф.

snatch.
piz-DYON-ku.
пиздёнку.

shaved pussy.
pye-LOT-ku BRI-ta-ya.
пелотку бритая.

unshaved pussy.
pye-LOT-ku nye-BRI-ta-ya.
пелотку небритая.

clitoris.
KLI-tor.
клитор.

clit.
SI-kyel.
сикель.

'toris.
PO-khot-nik.
похотник.

fun button.
ga-SHET-ku.
гашетку.

The inner thigh cream pie.
myezh-du-NOZH-no-ye pi-RO-zhe-no-ye
Междуножное пирожное

Damn, she has a forest down there!
blin, u nye-YO lyes tam ras-TYOT!
Блин, у нё лес там растёт!

I'm completely shaved.
ya POL-nost-yu BRI-ta-ya.
Я полностью бритая.

·····Sex positions and perversions
syek-su-AL-ni-ye po-ZI-tsii i iz-vra-SCHE-ni-ya
Сексуальные позиции и извращения

Sex in Russia is rapidly becoming more adventurous than the standard missionary position of days gone by. There is little taboo attached to watching the occasional skin flick, and women often seem to enjoy them even more than the guys. So make some popcorn, pop in some porn, and get your groove on.

Missionary
mis-si-o-NYER-ska-ya
Миссионерская

Guy on top
muzh-CHI-na SVYER-khu
Мужчина сверху

Girl on top
ZHEN-shi-na SVYER-khu
Женщина сверху

Legs in the air
GU-sar-ska-ya
Гусарская

Spoon position
PO-za SBO-ku
Поза сбоку
Also called ложечка (*LO-zhech-ka*).

69
shest-dye-SYAT DYE-vyat
Шестьдесят девять

Backdoor
PO-za po-ko-RI-tel-ya
Поза покорителя

I like to take it doggy-style.
ya lyu-BLYU sto-YAT RAK-om.
Я люблю стоять раком.
Sometimes also just called догги (*DOG-gi*).

Give me a golden shower.
SDYE-lai mnye zo-lo-TOI dozhd.
Сделай мне **золотой дождь**.

I'm into anal sex.
ya ta-SCHUS ot a-NAL-no-vo SYEK-sa.
Я тащусь от анального секса.

Let's do it in the butt.
da-VAI v PO-pu.
Давай в попу.

Let's take a trip from Istan-blow to Butt-apest.
da-VAI po-pu-tye-SHEST-vu-yem iz rot-ter-DA-ma v po-pyen-GA-gyen.
Давай попутешествуем из Роттердама в Попенгаген.
This means oral sex followed by anal sex; it is based on a pun on the words for "mouth" (рот) and "butt" (попа) and the city names Rotterdam and Copenhagen. This is kinda prison slangy-ish—normal people don't really say it—but I think it's hilarious.

Ménage à trois
SHVYED-ska-ya sye-MYA
Шведская семья
Literally, a "Swedish family," which kinda makes me wonder what the hell is going on in Sweden.

I wanna have a threesome with you and your sister.

ya kho-CHU syeks vtro-YOM s to-BOI i s tvo-YEI syes-TROI.

Я хочу секс втроём с тобой и с твоей сестрой.

Let's have an orgy.

da-VAI u-STRO-im OR-gi-yu.

Давай устроим оргию.

Group sex

Ggup-po-VU-kha

Групповуха

Other words you might hear meaning group sex include цирк (*tsirk*), эстафета (*es-ta-FYE-ta*), and карусель (*ka-ru-SYEL*).

We went to the sex shop, but didn't find any Spanish Fly.

mi kho-DI-li v syeks SHOP, no nye na-SHLI SHPAN-sku-yu MUSH-ku.

Мы ходили в **секс шоп**, но не нашли **шпанскую мушку**.

Let's watch some porn.

da-VAI po-SMO-trim por-NU-khu.

Давай посмотрим порнуху.

My turn-ons include big tits, midgets, and whipped cream.

me-NYA voz-bu-ZHDA-yut bol-SHI-ye SIS-ki, KAR-li-ki, i VZBI-ti-ye SLIV-ki.

Меня возбуждают большие сиськи, карлики, и взбитые сливки.

I'm into sadomasochism.

ya u-vlye-KA-yus sa-do-ma-zo-KHIZ-mom.

Я увлекаюсь **садомазохизмом**.

Got any handcuffs?

YEST u te-BYA na-RUCH-ni-ki?

Есть у тебя наручники?

·····Orgasm
or-GAZM
Оргазм

I'm cumming!
ya kon-CHA-yu!
Я кончаю!

You got cum all over my leg!
ti pro-LIL kon-CHI-nu na mo-YU NO-gu!
Ты пролил кончину на мою ногу!

Cum on my face!
KON-chi na mo-YO li-TSO!
Кончи на моё лицо!

He jizzed all over my bed!
on za-va-FLIL mnye vsyu pos-TYEL!
Он **завафлил** мне всю постель!

I've never seen so much semen in all my life!
ya ni-kog-DA v ZHIZ-ni nye VI-dye-la STOL-ko
SPYER-mi!
Я никогда в жизни не видела столько **спермы**!

Wow, I've never seen female ejaculation before!
UKH ti, ya ni-kog-DA RAN-she nye VI-dyel ZHEN-sku-
yu e-YA-ku-lya-tsi-yu!
Ух ты, я никогда раньше не видел **женскую эякуляцию**!

Holy shit, multiple orgasms!
YOB, E-to MNO-zhest-vye-nnii or-GAZM!
Ёб, это **множественный оргазм**!

·····Sluts and fuck buddies
BLYA-di i ye-bu-NI
Бляди и ебуны

Sometimes you're just looking for a good time. No shame in that.

You are such a temptress!
ti ta-KA-ya so-blaz-NI-tyel-nitsa!
Ты такая **соблазнительница**!

I'm only looking for a fuck buddy.
ya i-SCHU lish ye-bu-NA.
Я ищу лишь **ебуна**.

She's such a ho.
o-NA ta-KA-ya blyad.
Она такая **блядь**.

He cheated on me with some slut.
on mnye iz-mye-NIL s ka-KOI-to SHLU-khoi.
Он мне изменил с какой-то **шлюхой**.

She's an easy lay.
o-NA lye-GKA na pye-rye-DOK.
Она легка на передок.

I heard she's a total slut.
ya SLI-shal, chto o-NA voob-SCHE GRYEL-ka.
Я слышал, что она вообще **грелка**.

That ho is only into one-night stands.
E-to pod-STIL-ka TOL-ko LYU-bit syeks na od-NU noch.
Эта **подстилка** только любит секс на одну ночь.

She smacked me in the face when I called her a sleazy cunt.
o-NA da-LA mnye po-SCHO-chi-nu, kog-DA ya ye-YO naz-VAL piz-DOI s u-SHA-mi.
Она дала мне пощёчину, когда я её назвал **пиздой с ушами**.

My neighbor is a disgusting Peeping Tom.
moi so-SYED pro-TIV-nii so-blya-da-TAI.
Мой сосед противный **соблядатай**.

He's a male slut.
on blya-DUN.
Он **блядун**.

He's a total horn dog.
u nye-VO piz-do-ma-NI-ya.
У него **пиздомания**.

Man, that old guy in my building is such a pervert.
blin, E-tot sta-RIK v mo-YOM DO-mye ta-KOI iz-vra-SCHE-nyets.
Блин, этот старик в моём доме такой **извращенец**.

She found herself a new boy toy at the disco.
*o-NA na-SHLA se-BYE NO-vo-vo **KHA-kha-lya** na dis-ko-TYE-kye.*
Она нашла себе нового **хахаля** на дискотеке.

He's just some pickup I met at a club last night.
*on PRO-sto ka-KOI-to **bik-so-SYOM** s ko-TO-rim ya po-zna-KO-mi-las vche-RA v KLU-bye.*
Он просто какой-то **биксосьём** с которым я познакомилась вчера в клубе.

I went to a night club looking for some cheap meat.
*ya po-SHOL v noch-NOI klub v POI-skakh **ras-kla-DU-shki**.*
Я пошёл в ночной клуб в поисках **раскладушки**.

Are all Russian jokes about women who whore around while their husbands are on business trips?
*nye-u-ZHELI vsye RU-sski-ye a-nek-DO-ti o TOM, kak ZHEN-schi-ni **blya-DU-yut** kog-DA svo-I MU-zhya v ko-man-di-ROV-kye?*
Неужели все русские анекдоты о том, как женщины **блядуют** когда свои мужья в командировке?

·····Sexual problems
syek-su-AL-ni-ye pro-BLYE-mi
Сексуальные проблемы

I bought her dinner and she wouldn't even sleep with me.
ya ye-YO u-go-STIL U-zhi-nom a so MNOI DA-zhe nye pye-rye-spa-LA.
Я её угостил ужином, а она со мной даже не переспала.

She's really cold in bed.
*o-NA O-chen **kho-LOD-na-ya** v po-STYE-li.*
Она очень **холодная** в постели.

She may look all purty, but I heard she's frigid.
*o-NA MO-zhet i VI-gla-dit kra-SI-ven-ko, no ya SLI-shal, chto o-NA **fri-GID-na-ya**.*
Она может и выглядит красивенько, но я слышал, что она **фригидная**.

He dumped her because she doesn't put out.
on ye-YO BRO-sil po-to-MU chto o-NA nye da-YOT.
Он её бросил потому что она **не даёт**.

He's impotent.
on im-po-TYENT.
Он **импотент**.

She dumped him when he couldn't get it up.
o-NA ye-VO BRO-si-la, kog-DA u nye-VO nye sto-YAL.
Она его бросила, когда **у него не стоял**.

When he drinks he gets a softy.
kog-DA on pyot, u nye-VO nye-sto-YAK.
Когда он пьёт, у него **нестояк**.

·····Masturbation
o-na-NIZM
Онанизм

And if all else fails, it may be time to spank the ol' monkey. It's safe, it's cheap, and it won't expect you to pay for dinner.

I think I'm just going to sit home tonight and jack off.
na-VYER-no ya se-VOD-nya PRO-sto po-si-ZHU DO-ma i po-dro-CHU.
Наверно я сегодня просто посижу дома и **подрочу**.

When I can't find a girl, I just choke the chicken.
YES-li nye mo-GU nai-TI dyev-CHON-ku, ya PRO-sto LI-so-vo v ku-la-KYE go-NYU.
Если не могу найти девчонку, я просто **лысого в кулаке гоню**.

Every night I like to watch some porn and tune the violin.
KAZH-dii VYE-cher ya lyu-BLYU smo-TRYET por-NU-khu i na-STRA-i-vat SKRIP-ku.
Каждый вечер я люблю смотреть порнуху и **настраивать скрипку**.

What the hell do I need men for when I can get off with a vibrator?

*ka-KO-vo KHRYE-na mnye NA-do muzh-CHI-nu, kog-DA ya kai-FU-yu ot **vi-BRA-to-ra**?*

Какого хрена мне надо мужчину, когда я кайфую от **вибратора**?

That bean flipper just wants a new electric vibrator for her birthday.

*E-ta **ba-la-LAI-ka** TOL-ko KHO-chet NO-vii **e-lek-tro-SHTU-tser** na svoi dyen rozh-DYE-ni-ya.*

Эта **балалайка** только хочет новый **электроштуцер** на свой день рождения.

·····Prostitution

pro-sti-TU-tsi-ya
Проституция

If you're striking out, don't lose hope. As long as the provinces remain poor and the Ukrainian border stays open, whores in Russia will be plentiful and cheap. So where does one find a good whore in Russia? I'm glad you asked! There are tons of cruising strips (called *tochki*), brothels (*bordeli*), classified ads in expat newspapers, and high-end nightclubs and strip joints that can hook you up. And likely, your own hotel will even have an in-house supply ready, willing, and able to fulfill your every sick and twisted fantasy for a few greenbacks. If all else fails, just ask a cab driver where you can find a girl, and for a few extra bucks he will take you to the place. Here are some words you'll need to know to be a satisfied John.

Where can I find a…?

gdye MOZH-no na-i-TI…?
Где можно найти…?

These are all in the accusative.

prostitute
pro-sti-TUT-ku
проститутку

hooker
noch-NU-yu BA-boch-ku
ночную бабочку

whore
SHLYU-khu
шлюху

trick
shar-MU-tu
шармуту

tramp
sha-LA-vu
шалаву

slut
po-tas-KU-khu
потаскуху

streetwalker
U-lich-nu-yu FYE-yu
уличную фею

call girl
DYE-voch-ku po VI-zo-vu
девочку по вызову

lady of the night
ko-ro-LYE-vu po-lu-TMI
королеву полутьмы

young hooker
ba-TON-chik
батончик

Where's the nearest cruising strip?
gdye SA-ma-ya bli-ZHAI-sha-ya TOCH-ka?
Где самая ближайшая **точка**?
Sometimes also called a панель (*pa-NYEL*).

We got drunk and went whoring.
mi na-PI-lis i po-YE-kha-li kur-VYA-zhi-tsa.
Мы напились и поехали **курвяжиться**.

Pimp
su-te-NYOR
Сутенёр
When it comes to street prostitution, most of the pimps are part of either Chechen or Dagestani mafia groups, and they are some serious mofos. Don't fuck with them.

She had a shiner cuz her pimp beat her up.
*u nye-YO bil si-NYAK po-to-MU, chto **BAN-der** ye-YO iz-BIL.*
У неё был синяк потому, что **бандер** её избил.

The Madam is a skanky old bitch.
*E-ta **BAN-der-sha**—BLYAS-ska-ya, STA-ra-ya SU-ka.*
Эта **бандерша**—блядская старая сука.

John
cha-sov-SCHIK
Часовщик
Specifically one who pays by the hour.

Brothel
bor-DYEL
Бордель

Do you know a good whorehouse in Moscow?
*ti nye ZNA-yesh kho-RO-shii **tra-kho-DROM** v mosk-VYE?*
Ты не знаешь хороший **траходром** в Москве?

Hey, I ordered a blonde!
eh, a za-ka-ZAL blon-DIN-ku!
Ей, я заказал блондинку!

·····Negotiating a price
tor-GOV-lya po tse-NYE
Торговля по цене

If you're short on cash, stick to street prostitutes or, in real desperation, train stations, but set your expectations low. The whores at nightclubs might be a lot easier on the eyes, but they will cost you a pretty penny. Nevertheless, it is always worth negotiating a fair rate.

How much for an hour?
SKOL-ko za CHAS?
Сколько за час?

What can I get for a tenner?
*chto ya po-lu-CHU za **cher-VO-nyets***?
Что я получу за **червонец**?

I'll give ya a fifty for a blowjob.
*DAM tye **pol-TI-nnik** za mi-NYET.*
Дам те **полтинник** за минет.

How about some anal for cash?
*KHO-chesh a-NAL za **NAL**?*
Хочешь анал за **нал**?

How much are you willing to shell out for her?
*SKOL-ko ti za nye-YO go-TOV **ba-SHLYAT**?*
Сколько ты за неё готов **башлять**?

How about a C for a threesome?
*da-VAI **STOL-nik** za syeks vtro-YOM?*
Давай **стольник** за секс втроём?

Could you lower the price if I became a regular customer?
*ti nye **u-STU-pish** YES-li ya STA-nu po-sto-YA-nnim kli-YEN-tom?*
Ты не **уступишь** если я стану постоянным клиентом?

I can't afford that—could you go a little lower?
*mnye nye po kar-MA-nu—ti bi mo-GLA **po-dye-SHEV-le**?*
Мне не по карману—ты бы могла **подешевле**?

How about a small discount for a poor, lonely foreigner?
*kak na-SCHOT **MA-lyen-koi SKID-ki** dlya BYED-no-vo, o-di-NO-ko-vo i-no-STRAN-tsa?*
Как насчёт **маленькой скидки** для бедного, одинокого иностранца?

I'm outta dough, could you give me a freebee?
*u me-NYA la-VE za-KON-chi-los—ti bi nye mo-GLA dat
mnye **na SHA-ru**?*
У меня лавэ закончилось—ты бы не могла дать
мне **на шару**?

The answer will almost certainly be no, unless you are in
the smallest of villages where foreigners are still considered
somewhat exotic.

·····Contraceptives
pro-ti-vo-za-CHA-toch-ni-ye SRYED-stva
Противозачаточные средства

There is a Russian saying that states, "having sex with a
condom is like smelling flowers through a gas mask." While
not all Russian men are that categorical—or poetic—when
it comes to birth control, there can still be a lot of resis-
tance. Nevertheless, condoms of varied quality, color, and
expiration date are widely available throughout Russia, as
are various spermicidal suppositories (called свечи, *svechi*)
and other nasty things you would probably never want to
touch with your hands, much less any other part of your
anatomy. Abortion, however, is still the main form of birth
control, especially in the provinces.

Have you got a…?
YEST u te-BYA…?
Есть у тебя…?

condom
prye-zyer-va-TIV
презерватив

johnny
gon-DON
гондон
However, when this word refers to a person, it's something
more along the lines of a total douche bag.

rubber
ga-LO-sha
галоша

love glove
noch-NOI no-SOK
ночной носок

Trojan
bu-DYO-nov-ka
будёновка

raincoat
pa-ra-SHUT
парашют

jimmy hat
fran-TSUZ-ska-ya SHA-poch-ka
французская шапочка

dick shield
na-KHUI-nik
нахуйник

Don't worry, I'm on the pill.
nye pye-rye-zhi-VAI, ya ta-BLYET-ki pyu.
Не переживай, я таблетки пью.

·····Pregnancy
bye-RYE-mye-nnost
Беременность

I'm late.
u me-NYA za-DYER-zhka.
У меня задержка.

She's in the family way.
o-NA v po-lo-ZHE-nii.
Она в положении.

Honey, I'm pregnant with another man's baby.
*do-ro-GOI, ya **bye-RYE-mye-nna** ot dru-GO-vo muzh-CHI-ni.*
Дорогой, я **беременна** от другого мужчины.

He dumped her as soon as she got knocked up.
*on ye-YO BRO-sil, kak TOL-ko o-NA **za-lye-TYE-la**.*
Он её бросил, как только она **залетела**.

She's had five abortions already and is probably sterile now.
*o-NA u-ZHE SDYE-la-la pyat **a-BOR-tov** i na-VYER-no tye-PYER **byes-PLOD-na-ya**.*
Она уже сделала пять **абортов** и наверно теперь **бесплодная**.

·····STDs
be-pe-pe-PE
БППП

БППП stands for Болезни, передаваемые половым путем (*bo-LYEZ-ni, pye-rye-da-VA-ye-mi-ye po-lo-VIM pu-TYOM*), or sexually transmitted diseases. There are a lot of STDs floating around Russia, but that's not the scary part. The scary part is the astronomical rate at which HIV has spread over the past 10 years. It used to be restricted almost entirely to IV drug users and prostitutes, but in recent years it has started to seep into the general population. The thing is, testing isn't very common and many Russians are turned off by condoms, so there are a lot of people walking around who have no idea that they are infected. As for treatment, don't even ask. Even if good treatment were available, most Russians can't afford it. All in all, it is a tragedy still unfolding, and one that many Russians continue to deny even exists. Just something to think about.

I caught an STD from that bitch I was dating.
ya poi-MAL na KON-chik ot E-toi SU-ki, s ko-TO-roi ya vstrye-CHAL-sya.
Я **поймал на кончик** от этой суки, с которой я встречался.

That bastard gave me crabs!
E-ta SVO-loch pye-rye-DAL mnye man-da-VOSH-ku!
Эта сволочь передал мне **мандавошку**!

It hurts when I piss—I think I have the clap again.
bo-LIT, kog-DA ya PI-sa-yu—po-MO-ye-mu u me-NYA o-PYAT gu-SAR-skii NAS-mork.
Болит, когда я писаю—по-моему у меня опять **гусарский насморк**.

I got a strange rash on my dick—I hope it's not herpes.
u me-NYA STRA-nna-ya sip na khu-YE—na-DYE-yus, E-to nye GYER-pyes.
У меня странная сыпь на хуе—надеюсь, это не **герпес**.

Do you need a prescription for penicillin in Russia?
NU-zhen li rye-TSEPT dlya pye-ni-tsi-LLI-na v ro-SSII?
Нужен ли рецепт для **пенициллина** в России?

Where can I find a doctor who treats venereal disease?
gdye MOZH-no na-i-TI vra-CHA, ko-TO-rii LYE-chit vye-nye-RI-ches-ki-ye bo-LYEZ-ni?
Где можно найти врача, который лечит **венерические болезни**?

I heard he's HIV infected.
ya SLI-shal, chto on vich-in-fi-TSI-ro-van.
Я слышал, что он **ВИЧ – инфицирован**.

He was sick for a long time, and they finally discovered he had AIDS.
on DOL-go bo-LYEL i na-ko-NYETS ob-na-RU-zhi-li, chto u nye-VO spid.
Он долго болел и наконец обнаружили, что у него **СПИД**.

•••••Gays
go-lu-BI-ye
Голубые

Despite the appearance in recent years of gay clubs and even a gay pride parade in Moscow, being out is not "in" in Russia. There is still a lot of discrimination against homosexuals, especially in smaller towns, and unfortunately hate crimes are still a reality. In other words, this is probably one of those places where it's better to keep a low profile unless you're around people you really know are cool with it.

There's actually a very elaborate system of gay slang in Russia, so here we're just going to give you some of the most basic, common words you might encounter while livin' la vida homo in Russia. Be careful of using some of these terms if you're not a member of the LGBTQ community or if you're with strangers, as some of these terms can be offensive.

Homosexual
go-mo-syeks-u-a-LIST
Гомосексуалист
This is a neutral term.

Gay
go-lu-BOI
Голубой
Also a fairly neutral term which, in most other contexts, means "light blue." It is also common to hear the English word "gay" (гей) being used these days.

Pederast
pye-de-RAST
Педераст
The retort to this is гетераст (*gye-te-RAST*), gay slang for a breeder.

Homo
GO-mik
Гомик

Queen
ar-MYAN-ska-ya ko-ro-LYE-va
Армянская королева
Literally, "Armenian queen," but it is used to refer to queens of all ethnicities.

Cruiser
shtri-kho-VA-ya DYEV-ka
Штриховая девка

Fairy
bak-TYE-ri-ya
Бактерия

Twinkie
bar-KHOT-ka
Бархотка
Cuz he's so soft and velvety.

Chicken
PYER-sik
Персик
Literally, a "little peach."

Chickenhawk
ko-SHOL-ka s va-zye-LI-nom
Кошёлка с вазелином
Literally, a "bag of Vaseline."

Rentboy
BYEL-ka
Белка
Literally, a "squirrel."

Black queer
man-DYE-lla
Манделла

Fat queer
BA-dya
Бадья

Closet case
pod-POL-schik
Подпольщик

Pitcher
DYA-tel
Дятел
Literally, a "woodpecker."

Receiver
pye-TUKH
Петух
Literally, a "rooster." Or perhaps "cock" is more apt.

Manwich
bu-ter-BROD
Бутерброд
In other words, a gay threesome.

Drag queen
trans-FOR-mer
Трансформер

Outter
kha-BAL-ka
Хабалка

Gay basher
rye-MONT-nik
Ремонтник

I'd really like to go to a gay club.
*mnye bi O-chen kho-TYE-los po-i-TI v **gei KLUB**.*
Мне бы очень хотелось пойти в **гей клуб**.

Moscow has a pretty active gay scene.
*v mosk-VYE do-STA-toch-no ak-TIV-na-ya **go-lu-BYAT-nya**.*
В Москве достаточно активная **голубятня**.

Where is the best cruising street in this city?
*gdye SA-ma-ya LU-chsha-ya **PLYE-shka** v E-tom GO-ro-dye?*
Где самая лучшая **плешка** в этом городе?
Also sometimes called панель (*pa-NYEL*)

Every big city has a queer quarter.
*v KAZH-dom bol-SHOM GO-ro-dye yest **go-mo-DROM**.*
В каждом большом городе есть **гомодром**.

Lesbian
lyes-bi-YAN-ka
Лесбиянка

Lesbo
LYES-ba
Лесба

Carpet muncher
LI-za
Лиза

A newbie vagitarian
nu-lye-VA-ya GYOR-la
Нулевая гёрла
Literally, a "zero girl."

Could you tell me the way to the nearest taco stand?
*ti mnye nye pod-SKA-zhesh, kak do-BRAT-sya do bli-ZHAI-shevo **LYES-bi-scha**?*
Ты мне не подскажешь, как добраться до ближайшего **лесбища**?

CHAPTER 6

ANGRY RUSSIAN

ZLOI RU-SSKII
Злой русский

Or, How to Get Your Ass Kicked in Russia.

If you spend even a short amount of time in Russia, sooner or later someone is gonna piss you off. Choose your words carefully though, as alcohol + pissed-off Russian = a situation that could escalate unexpectedly fast. If you're ready to put your money where your mouth is and you're crazy enough to see it through to the bitter end, here you go. *Udachi!*

🍸 RED RUSSIAN

After getting slapped around by your frenemies, drink something that will match the bruises on your face.

GET THESE:
2 ounces vodka
2 ounces cherry liqueur
cherry, for garnish

DO THIS:
Put the vodka and cherry liqueur in a glass with ice. Stir until it's well chilled, then garnish with a cherry. The ice-cold glass can be held against any bruises on your face in between sips.

•••••You talkin' to me?

ti MNYE go-vo-RISH?

Ты мне говоришь?

Hey buddy, what's the problem?
eh, dru-ZHOK, chto za pro-BLYE-ma?
Эй, дружок, что за проблема?

What's the deal?
v chom DYE-lo?
В чём дело?

What are you messing with me for?
cho ti pri-sta-YOSH?
Чё ты пристаёшь?

What the hell is going on here?
chto za BLYAD-stvo?
Что за блядство?

What is this mess?
chto za bar-DAK?
Что за бардак?

What is this nonsense?
cho E-to za bai-DA?
Чё это за байда?

Stop your frontin'!
nye vi-PYEN-dri-vaj-sya!
Не выпендривайся!

What, have you lost your mind?
u tebya CHTO, KRI-sha po-YE-kha-la?
У тебя что, **крыша поехала**?

What the hell do you want, you little shit?
CHO tye NA-do, gav-NYUK?
Чё те надо, гавнюк?

•••••Get outta my face!

s glaz do-LOI!

С глаз долой!

Piss off!
i-DI ti NA fig!
Иди ты на фиг!

Go to hell!
i-DI k CHOR-tu!
Иди к чёрту!

Shove off!
po-SHOL ti!
Пошёл ты!

I've had it up to here with you!
ya to-BOI sit po GOR-lo!
Я тобой сыт по горло!

I've fucking had it with you!
ti me-NYA za-ye-BAL!
Ты меня заебал!

I'm so damn fed up with you already!
ti me-NYA za-dol-BAL u-ZHE!
Ты меня задолбал уже!

I'm sick of your stupid mug!
mnye na-do-YE-la tvo-YA du-RATS-ka-ya RO-zha!
Мне надоела твоя дурацкая рожа!

Get outta here, bitch!
va-LI ot-SYU-da, SU-ka!
Вали отсюда, сука!

Get your sorry ass outta here!
che-SHI BUL-ka-mi ot-SYU-da!
Чеши булками отсюда!

Get the fuck away from me!
ot-ye-BIS ot me-NYA!
Отъебись от меня!

Get your hands off me!
RU-ki PROCH ot me-NYA!
Руки прочь от меня!

Leave me alone!
o-STAV me-NYA v po-KO-ye!
Оставь меня в покое!

Move your ass!
PIZ-dui!
Пиздуй!

I ain't got time for you!
mnye nye do te-BYA sei-CHAS!
Мне не до тебя сейчас!

Don't even think you can dis me like that.
DA-zhe nye DU-mai, chto MO-zhesh me-NYA khui nye STA-vit.
Даже не думай, что можешь **меня в хуй не ставить**.

Don't try to screw me over.
nye sta-RAI-sya me-NYA vyer-TYET na ba-NA-nye.
Не старайся меня **вертеть на банане**.

Stop trying to pull a fast one on me!
KHVA-tit mo-RO-zi-tsya!
Хватит **морозиться**!

Don't try to pull one over on me!
nye PU-dri mnye moz-GI!
Не пудри мне мозги!

Don't play me for an idiot!
nye DYEL-ai iz me-NYA i-di-O-ta!
Не делай из меня идиота!

What, are you trying to rip me off?
ti CHO, KHO-chesh ob-o-DRAT me-NYA kak LI-pu?
Ты чё, хочешь **ободрать меня как липу**?

If you touch me again, my husband's gonna kick your ass.

*YES-li ye-SCHO raz me-NYA TRO-nyesh, muzh **te-BYE piz-dyu-LEI na-VYE-sha-yet**.*

Если ещё раз меня тронешь, муж **тебе пиздюлей навешает**.

Stop giving me the third!

KHVA-tit me-NYA mu-RI-zhit!

Хватит меня **мурыжить**!

Don't screw around!

nye BA-lui-sya!

Не балуйся!

Don't tell me a bunch of jive!

nye ras-SKA-zi-vai mnye BAI-ki!

Не рассказывай мне байки!

·····Fuck off!
po-SHOL ti NA khui!
Пошёл ты на хуй!

This is the most common way to tell someone to fuck off. Keep in mind that the form has to change if you're talking to a chick (пошла ты на хуй!) or to a group of people (пошли вы на хуй!). Although this one phrase will always take you where you wanna go, if you like a little variety in your curs-

---

DAMN!)))
CHORT!
ЧЁРТ

Darn!	*blin!*	Блин!
Damn!	*blyad!*	Блядь!
Dammit!	*BLA-kha MU-kha!*	Бляха муха!
Oh, snap!	*YO mo-YO!*	Ё моё!
Goddammit!	*chort voz-MI!*	Чёрт возьми!
Well, shoot!	*YOL-ki PAL-ki!*	Ёлки палки!
Fucking shit!	*ye-BA-tsa-SRA-tsa!*	Ебаться-сраться!
Fuck!	*piz-DYETZ!*	Пиздец!

ing, here are some other phrases you can use with more or less the same general meaning.

Fuck you!
YOB te-BYA!
Ёб тебя!

Fuck your mother!
YOB tvo-YU mat!
Ёб твою мать!

Fuck no!
khui v rot!
Хуй в рот!

Go fuck yourself!
i-DI v ZHO-pu!
Иди в жопу!
Literally, "go to ass."

What the fuck!
na khu-YU VI-dyet!

На хую видеть!

Fuck you in the mouth!
ye-BAT te-BYA v rot!
Ебать тебя в рот!

F you!
po-SHOL na tri BUK-vi!
Пошёл на три буквы!

While most Russians do understand the gesture of giving the bird, they also have a gesture called the фиг (*fig*), which is used in the same way but is formed by making a fist and putting your thumb between your index and middle finger. For example:

He gave me the fig.
on dal mnye fig.
Он дал мне фиг.
In other words, he flipped me off Russian style.

NAME CALLIN')))

OB-ZI-VA-NI-YE
ОБЗЫВАНИЕ

Bitch!
SU-ka!
Сука!
(used for both
males and females)

Son of a bitch!
SU-kin sin!
Сукин сын!

Bastard!
PAD-la!
Падла!

Dummy!
ba-RAN!
Баран

Wacko!
byez-BA-she-nnii!
Безбашенный!

Asshole!
mu-DAK!
Мудак

Jackass!
ko-ZYOl!
Козёл!

Freak!
u-ROD!
Урод!

Prick!
pod-LYETS!
Подлец!

Dirty ass prick!
khui nye-MI-tii
Хуй немытый!

Scumbag!
po-DO-nok!
Подонок!

Dipshit!
lokh!
Лох!

Moron!
dye-BIL!
Дебил!

Psycho!
psikh!
Псих!

Cocksucker!
khu-ye-SOS!
Хуесос!

Fucking whore!
BLYAD-ska-ya piz-do-YO-bi-na!
Блядская пиздоёбина!

Fuck brain!
moz-go-YOB!
Мозгоёб!

Trainstation whore!
SHLYU-kha vok-ZAL-na-ya!
Шлюха вокзальная!

Ass-eyed cunt!
piz-DA zho-po-GLA-za-ya!
Пизда жопоглазая!

Fucking bitch!
SU-ka zlo-ye-BU-cha-ya!
Сука злоебучая!

Fucking piece of shit!
YO-ba-nnii za-SRA-nyets!
Ёбанный засранец!

·····Talkin' shit

ob-si-RA-ni-ye
Обсирание

Don't be a smart aleck!
nye UM-ni-chai!
Не умничай!

Stop being such a wanker!
KHVA-tit kha-MIT!
Хватит хамить!

Don't ask me such stupid questions!
nye za-da-VAI mnye du-RATS-ki-kh vo-PRO-sov!
Не задавай мне дурацких вопросов!

Shut your piehole!
past za-KHLOP-ni!
Пасть захлопни!

Shut up, you fucking moron!
zat-KNIS, dol-bo-YOB!
Заткнись, долбоёб!

Shut your fucking mouth already!
zat-KNI ye-BA-lo u-ZHE!
Заткни ебало уже!

Drop dead!
chtob ti SDOKH!
Чтоб ты сдох!

Eat shit and die!
zhri gov-NO i SDOKH-ni!
Жри говно и сдохни!

Shove it up your ass!
khui te-BYE v ZHO-pu!
Хуй тебе в жопу!

You stinking bastard!
u-BLYU-dok vo-NYU-chii!
Ублюдок вонючий!

·····Kickin' ass

mor-do-BOI
Мордобой

When it's time to really get your game on and make your ass-kicking intentions known, these phrases won't leave 'em guessing about how the night is gonna end. So get out your brass knuckles, update your insurance policy, and let's rumble Russian style!

What, you cruisin' for a bruisin'?
*ti CHTO, **KHO-chesh MA-khach**?*
Ты что, **хочешь махач**?

I'm gonna kick your ass!
ya te-BYA vye-BYU!
Я тебя въебу!

I'll crack your nuts wide open!
ya te-BYE SDYE-la-yu YICH-ni-tsu!
Я тебе сделаю яичницу!
Literally, "I'll make you scrambled eggs." If you recall, in Russian, balls are called "eggs."

I'm going to kill you!
ya te-BYA GROKH-nu!
Я тебя грохну!

I'm gonna ice you!
ya te-BYA za-mo-CHU!
Я тебя замочу!

If you come near me again, I'm gonna open up a can of whoop ass on you!
*YES-li ye-SCHO raz ko MNYE po-do-i-DYOSH, ya te-BYA **pye-rre-khu-YA-ryu**!*
Если ещё раз ко мне подойдёшь, я тебя **перехуярю**!

If you don't shut your mouth, I'm gonna beat the shit out of you!
*YES-li nye za-KRO-yesh rot, ya te-BYA **ot-PI-zhu**!*
Если не закроешь рот, я тебя **отпизжу**!

RACIAL SLURS)))

RA-SIST-SKI-YE VI-RA-ZHE-NI-YA

РАСИСТСКИЕ ВЫРАЖЕНИЯ

There ain't nothin' PC about Russian culture, and everything from nasty racial and ethnic slurs to the ubiquitous *Chukchi* jokes are fairly common. Chukchi are an indigenous people of the Russian Far Eastern District, and if you've never heard a *Chukcha* joke, they're usually something along these lines.

> **Why does the Chukcha open yogurt in the store?**
> **Because it says "Open here"!**
>
> *po-che-MU CHUK-cha ot-kri-VA-yet YO-gurt v ma-ga-ZI-nye?*
> *po-to-MU chto na nyom na-PI-sa-no: "Ot-KRIT zdyes"!*
> Почему чукча открывает йогурт в магазине?
> Потому что на нем написано: "Открыть здесь"!

In other words, like most racist humor, this ain't real clever stuff.

BLACKASS
CHYER-NO-ZHO-PII

ЧЕРНОЖОПЫЙ

This term describes not only people of African descent, but basically anyone darker skinned than your average Slav, such as Caucasians (i.e., people from the Caucasus region). Here's a little irony for you: In the U.S., a "Caucasian" is a white person, but to a Russian a "Caucasian" is black. Go figure. You might also hear the term черномазый (*hyer-no-MA-zii*) referring to any dark-skinned person. Black people of African origin are usually called негры (*NYE-gri*), which is actually considered a fairly neutral term, unlike its English equivalent.

LKN
el-ka-EN

ЛКН

This stands for лицо кавказкой национальности (*li-TSO kav-KAZ-koi na-sti-o-NAL-nos-ti*), or a person of Caucasian nationality. There is in fact no such thing as a single "Caucasian nationality," and this term can refer to anyone from Armenians, Georgians, and Azeris to Chechens, Ingush, and various ethnic groups of Dagestan.

CAUCASIAN
KHA-CHIK

ХАЧИК

Again, meaning someone from the Caucasus region. This term comes from an Armenian name.

CENTRAL ASIAN
U-RYUK

УРЮК

> You might also hear чурбан (*chur-BAN*) or чурка (*CHUR-ka*)

UKRAINIAN
KHO-KHOL

ХОХОЛ

> A female Ukrainian is a хохлушка (*kho-KHLUSH-ka*), and Ukraine itself is sometimes referred to as Хохландия (*khokh-LAN-di-ya*).

BELARUSIAN
BUL-BASH

БУЛЬБАШ

YID
ZHID

ЖИД

> Israel is also sometimes referred to as Жидовия (*zhi-DO-vi-ya*). You may also here the words зяма (*ZYA-ma*) and Рабинович (*ra-bi-NO-vich*) in reference to Jews.

SLIT EYE
UZ-KO-GLA-ZII

УЗКОГЛАЗЫЙ

FROG
LYA-GU-SCHAT-NIK

ЛЯГУШАТНИК

> Funny how everyone seems to call them that.

YANK
A-ME-RI-KOS

АМЕРИКОС

> You may also hear, ЮС (*yus*) from "U.S.", and, of course Янки (*YAN-ki*). There is also the word ПИНДОС (*pin-DOS*), which used to apply to American military serving abroad, but is now often used for Americans in general.

RUSSKY
MOS-KAL

МОСКАЛЬ

> This term is mainly used by Ukrainians to refer to their sometimes not-so-friendly neighbors. You might also hear русак (*ru-SAK*) and кацап (*ka-TSAP*).

You want a piece of this?
*ti CHO, **KHO-chesh piz-DI po-lu-CHIT**?*
Ты чё, **хочешь пизды получить**?

On your knees, bitch!
na ko-LYE-ni, SU-ka!
На колени, сука!

I'm going to rearrange your face!
ya te-BYE na-CHI-schu RI-lo!
Я тебе начищу рыло!

I'm gonna fuck you up!
ya te-BYA iz-mu-DO-kha-yu!
Я тебя измудохаю!

I'm going to bash your fuckin' face in!
ya te-BYE VRYE-zhu po ye-BA-lu!
Я тебе врежу по ебалу!

I'm gonna own you, bitch!
ya te-BYA VI-ye-blyu, SU-ka!
Я тебя выеблю, сука!

·····Relax!
ras-SLAB-sya!
Расслабься!

And if you wuss out at the last minute…

Calm down!
us-po-KOI-sya!
Успокойся!

Get a grip!
voz-MI se-BYA v RU-ki!
Возьми себя в руки!

Come to your senses!
o-POM-nis!
Опомнись!

Everything's under control here.
VSYO tut pod kon-TROL-yem.
Всё тут под контролем.

No questions/I got it.
ba-ZA-rov nyet.
Базаров нет.

Whatever you say.
kak SKA-zhesh.
Как скажешь.

·····Indifference
rav-no-DU-shi-ye
Равнодушие

They say the opposite of love isn't hate; it's indifference. So if you really wanna piss someone off, just tell them how little you care.

I don't give a care.
mnye PO fi-gu.
Мне по фигу.

I couldn't care less.
mnye po ba-ra-BA-nu.
Мне по барабану.

I don't give a shit.
mnye na-SRAT.
Мне насрать.

I don't give a damn.
mnye na-plye-VAT.
Мне наплевать.

Makes no diff to me.
da mnye ab-so-LYUT-no fi-o-LYE-to-vo.
Да мне абсолютно фиолетово.

I don't give a rat's ass.
mnye PO-khui.
Мне похуй.

I don't give a fuck.
me-NYA E-to nye ye-BYOT.
Меня это не ебёт.

What the hell do I need your problems for?
na fi-GA mnye nuzh-NI tvo-I pro-BLYE-mi?
На фига мне нужны твои проблемы?

What the hell do I care?
nu, a mnye ka-KOI khryen?
Ну, а мне какой хрен?

And what do I have to do with it?
a ya tut pri-CHOM?
А я тут причём?

That's all I need!
TOL-ko E-to-vo mnye nye khva-TA-yet!
Только этого мне не хватает!

To fuck with it all!
ye-BIS vsyo ko-NYOM!
Ебись всё конём!

·····Smack talk
vsyAkaya gAdost
Всякая гадость

I don't know what it is about talking shit about other people, but it just feels good. Mocking others is actually one
of my favorite pastimes. From ridiculing friends and family
members to total strangers, it's good, clean fun to grossly
exaggerate—if not outright fabricate—various personal
weaknesses for your own entertainment.

He's a liar.
on vrun.
Он врун.

He always talks nonsense.
on po-sto-YA-nno bryed nye-SYOT.
Он постоянно бред несёт.

He thinks he's all that.
on schi-TA-yet se-BYA kru-TIM.
Он считает себя крутым.

He's not only a moron, but he smells bad, too.
*on nye TOL-ko **dye-BIL**, on ye-SCHO **i von-YA-yet**.*
Он не только **дебил**, он ещё и **воняет**.

His hot ride totally means that he has a tiny dick.
ye-VO KLASS-na-ya TACH-ka od-no-ZNACH-no go-vo-RIT o tom, chto u nye-VO MA-lyen-kii chlyen.
Его классная тачка однозначно говорит о том, что у него **маленький член**.

What, can't you see he just a screwball?
ti CHTO, nye VI-dish, chto E-to zhe KLO-un?
Ты что, не видишь, что это же **клоун**?

He does everything half assed.
on vsyo DYEL-a-yet v pyen ko-LO-du.
Он всё делает **в пень колоду**.

Her tits gotta be fake.
ye-YO SIS-ki TOCH-no si-li-KO-no-vi-ye.
Её сиськи точно силиконовые.

Her ass is way too fat for those jeans.
ye-YO ZHO-pa SLISH-kom TOL-sta-ya dlya ta-KIKH JIN-sov.
Её **жопа слишком толстая** для таких джинсов.

He's the biggest dickhead I have ever seen.
ta-KO-vo VSHI-vo-vo piz-DYU-ka ya ye-SCHO nye vi-DAL.
Такого **вшивого пиздюка** я ещё не видал.

Just look at that loser—what a freak!
ti po-smo-TRI na E-to-vo LU-ze-ra—ta-KOI u-ROD!
Ты посмотри на этого **лузера**—такой урод!

He's a fucking zero.
on vo-ob-SCHE piz-do-YOB.
Он **вообще пиздоёб**.

He's a total bastard and a real smart-ass to boot.
on po-SLYED-nya-ya SVO-loch i k to-MU zhe ta-KOI khi-tro-ZHO-pii.
Он **последняя сволочь** и к тому же такой **хитрожопый**.

He's such a douche bag and I'm sick of all his frontin'.
on ta-KOI gon-DON i mnye na-do-YE-li ye-VO pon-TI.
Он такой **гондон** и мне надоели его **понты**.

She's such an idiot.
*o-NA ta-KA-ya **DU-ra**.*
Она такая **дура**.

She's such a wench.
*o-NA ta-KA-ya **STYER-va**.*
Она такая **стерва**.

I'm sick of her bitchiness.
*mnye na-do-YE-la ye-YO **VRYED-nost**.*
тне надоела её **вредность**.

She's just a skanky blonde bimbo.
*o-NA PROS-to BLYAD-ska-ya **bye-lo-KUR-va**.*
Она просто блядская **белокурва**.

She's so easy she changes lovers more often than she changes her underwear.
o-NA ta-KA-ya da-VAL-ka, chto mye-NYA-yet lyu-BV-ni-kov CHA-sche, chem svo-I TRU-si-ki.
Она такая давалка, что меняет любовников чаще, чем свои трусики.

He thinks he's hot shit.
*on chi-TA-yet se-BYA **khu-YOM VAZH-nim**.*
Он считает себя **хуём важным**.

He's kind of a weirdo.
u nye-VO ta-ra-KA-ni v go-lo-VYE.
У него тараканы в голове.
Literally, "he's got cockroaches in his head."

He throws his scratch away on schlock.
on vi-BRA-si-va-yet svo-YO ba-BLO na ba-ra-KHLO.
Он выбрасывает своё бабло на барахло.

He always takes the bus because he's such a tightwad.
*on vseg-DA YEZ-dit na av-TO-bu-sye po-to-MU chto **ye-VO ZHA-ba DU-shit**.*
Он всегда ездит на автобусе, потому что его **жаба душит**.
The image is literally of someone being strangled by a toad.

She belongs in a psych ward.
*ye-YO MYE-sto—**v psi-KHUSH-kye**.*
Её место—**в психушке**.

I'm cheesed by…

me-NYA BYE-sit (singular)…/me-NYA BYE-syat (plural)…

Меня бесит…/Меня бесят…

> **your idiotic grin.**
> *tvo-YA i-di-OT-ska-ya u-LIB-ka.*
> твоя идиотская улыбка.

> **your stanky armpits.**
> *tvo-I vo-NYU-chi-ye pod-MIH-ki.*
> твои вонючие подмышки.

> **your slutty girlfriend.**
> *tvo-YA BLYAD-ska-ya po-DRUZH-ka.*
> твоя блядская подружка.

> **your stupid ideas.**
> *tvo-I du-RAT-ski-ye i-dye-I.*
> твои дурацкие идеи.

> **your endless jabber.**
> *tvo-YA byes-ko-NYECH-na-ya bol-tov-NYA.*
> твоя бесконечная болтовня.

·····Disbelief

nye-do-VYER-i-ye

Недоверие

Let's face it: Most people are full of crap. I say, call them out and tell them straight up that you ain't buyin' what they're sellin'.

> **You gotta be kidding me!**
> *da ti chto!*
> Да ты что!

> **That's hogwash!**
> *in-tye-RYES-no-ye ki-NO!*
> Интересное кино!

> **What a load of crap!**
> *chto za **che-pu-KHA**!*
> Что за **чепуха**!

> **That's total BS!**
> *E-to POL-nii bryed!*
> Это полный бред!

That's bull!
E-to ga-LI-ma!
Это **галимо**!

That's doggy doo!
E-to chuzh so-BA-chya!
Это чушь собачья!

That's nonsense!
E-to NON-sens!
Это **нонсенс**!

Don't try to play me.
nye NA-do mnye lap-SHU na U-shi VYE-shat
Не надо мне лапшу на уши вешать.
Literally, "don't hang noodles from my ears." Now just try to tell me that Russian isn't the coolest language ever.

That's a total joke!
vot E-to pri-KOL!
Вот это прикол!

That's nuts!
s u-MA so-i-TI!
С ума сойти!

This is a madhouse!
E-to dur-DOM!
Это **дурдом**!

·····Mafia speak
BO-tat po FYE-nye
Ботать по фене

When most people think of the Russian Mafia, they think of flat-headed thugs who drive black Beemers and throw money around on strippers and slot machines. But Russian organized crime wasn't always so flashy. The most respected figure of the Russian underworld has always been the вор в законе (*vor v za-KO-nye*), or "thief in law." These guys are serious badasses, but with a very strict code of behavior that has traditionally prevented them from running amuck as the rank-and-file Mafia thugs do today. They also have a language all their own—called блатной жаргон (*blat-NOI zhar-GON*) or воровской жаргон (*vo-ro-VSKOI zhar-GON*)—which thrived in prisons and the camps of Siberia. Nowadays, though, this language has seeped out to the general population, particularly to those who want to send a clear don't-fuck-with-me message. Vladimir Putin himself is known for occasionally tossing out a little criminal slang, especially when talking about Chechen.

Sadly, this colorful language is not for you to use, dear foreigner: There are some places you just don't go unless you have the cultural cred of a native. Nonetheless, I've included some phrases you may come across at some point and some that I just think are cool.

> **They say there's a new crime syndicate controlling the south side.**
> *go-vo-RYAT, chto NO-va-ya gru-ppi-ROV-ka kon-tro-LI-ru-yet YUZH-nii rai-ON.*
> Говорят, что новая **группировка** контролирует южный район.
>
> **Any double-crosser better get ready to meet his maker.**
> *lyu-BOI krot DOL-zhen za-KA-zi-vat SA-van.*
> Любой **крот** должен **заказывать саван**.
>
> **If I find out who the sellout is, I'm gonna eliminate him.**
> *YES-li ya uz-NA-yu kto tut SHKU-ra, ya ye-VO u-da-LYU.*
> Если я узнаю кто тут **шкура**, я его **удалю**.

I'll head butt you in the teeth if you don't **watch your mouth.**

*ya te-BYE **pri-MU kal-GAN**, YES-li nye **slye-DISH za myet-LOI**.*

Я тебе **приму калган**, если не **следишь за метлой**.

I'll cut your throat if you **show up** on our **turf** again.

*ya pye-rye-RYE-zhu te-BYE GOR-lo, YES-li ye-SCHO raz **na-ri-SU-yesh-sya** na NA-shei **TOCH-kye**.*

Я перережу тебе горло, если ещё раз **нарисуешься** на нашей **точке**.

I thought he was my **paisano,** but he turned out to be a **rat.**

*ya DU-mal, chto on mnye **kyent**, no o-ka-ZAL-sya **KRI-soi**.*

Я думал, что он мне **кент**, но оказался **крысой**.

They **put a contract out** on that **blabbermouth.**

*o-NI **za-ka-ZA-li tran-DU**.*

Они **заказали транду**.

He got **rubbed out** in the **john.**

*ye-VO **val-NU-li** v dal-nya-KYE.*

Его **вальнули в дальняке**.

After he got **sent up the river**, the **pickpocket** decided to **change his prof.**

*PO-sle to-VO, kak ye-VO **po-SLA-li na ot-SID-ku**, **schi-PACH** rye-SHIL **me-NYAT o-KRAS-ku**.*

После того, как его **послали на отсидку**, **щипач** решил **менять окраску**.

He **croaked** in the **big house.**

*on **KRYAK-nul** v **KI-che**.*

Он **крякнул в киче**.

Don't **run your mouth** around **the boss.**

*ne NA-do **bu-ro-VIT** u **av-to-ri-TYE-ta**.*

Не надо **буровить у авторитета**.

If you see a **panda bear**, hide your **piece** and **scram!**

*YES-li u-VI-dish **vo-ro-NOK**, pryach **zhe-LYE-zo**, i ka-NAI ot-TU-da!*

Если увидишь **воронок**, прячь **железо**, и канай оттуда!

I heard that there was another gang rape last night.
ya SLI-shal, chto vche-RA o-PYAT KI-nu-li na bri-GA-du.
Я слышал, что вчера опять **кинули на бригаду**.

Say your prayers before I put a cap in your gourd.
mazh lob zye-LYEN-koi, po-KA ya nye STA-vil o-RYEKH v tvo-YU TIK-vu.
Мажь лоб зеленкой, пока я не ставил **орех** в твою **тыкву**.

He got sprung from the pen by his connections.
on po-lu-CHIL cko-SCHU-khu po BLA-tu.
Он получил **скощуху** по **блату**.
Po blatu is one of those phrases that has come to be commonly used, even by respectable folks, when talking about getting something through a network of influential connections.

After they put the bracelets on him, they sent him up the river.
POS-le to-VO, kak ye-VO za-KO-tsa-li, ye-VO za-KRI-li.
После того, как его **закоцали**, его **закрыли**.

He sat out his term and then returned to back to his gang.
on ot-ru-BIL ot zvon-KA do zvon-KA i vyer-NUL-sya k svo-YEI SHAI-kye.
Он **отрубил от звонка до звонка** и вернулся к своей **шайке**.

He was a real good guy, but he fucked up royally, and now he's a goner.
on bil or-LOM, no ko-so-RYE-zil i tye-PYER ye-MU kran-TI.
Он был **орлом**, но **косорезил** и теперь ему **кранты**.

They sent him to Sochi for always being a dumbass.
ye-VO ot-PRA-vi-li v SO-chi za TO, chto po-sto-YA-nno bi-ko-VAL.
Его **отправили в Сочи** за то, что постоянно **быковал**.
In other words, they killed him.

They didn't know what happened to him until they found the corpsicle.

o-NI nye ZNA-li, chto s nim slu-CHI-los po-KA nye na-SHLI pod-SNYEZH-nik.

Они не знали, что с ними случилось пока не нашли **подснежник**.

A *podsnyezhnik* is literally a snowdrop—you know, that flower that begins to appear just as the winter snow is starting to melt. Therefore, this slang use refers to corpses that begin to appear with the first thaw of spring. Kinda pretty, ain't it?

The hitman didn't lose his cool when he saw the blue light special coming.

myas-NIK nye shu-GAL-sya kog-DA u-VI-dyel si-nye-GLAZ-ku.

Мясник не **шугался** когда увидел **синеглазку**.

You'll also frequently hear the word киллер (*KI-ller*) to refer to a hitman. Keep in mind that in Russian this means specifically someone hired to kill someone on contract, not just someone who kills in general, as it does in English.

One last phrase you should know is в натуре (*v na-TUR-ye*). This translates something like "really," "totally," or "in fact." You know when you make fun of stoners and overuse the filler "like"? Well, when Russians make fun of goons, they toss around the phrase в натуре. *I eto, tipa, chisto v naturye, bratan.*

CHAPTER 7

POPPY RUSSIAN

POP-SO-VII RU-SSKII
Попсовый русский

There's no denying it: Russian pop music sucks. Fortunately, there are a number of decent alternative and hard-core bands to make up for it. In terms of language, you'll probably be happy to know that the vast majority of words related to music and pop culture in Russia are just English words pronounced with a Russified accent. So really the more English you speak when discussing topics of pop culture, the hipper you'll sound.

·····Musical Genres
mu-zi-KALni-ye ZHAN-ri
Музыкальные жанры

Let's listen to some…
Da-VAI po-SLUsha-yem…
Давай послушаем…

God I hate…
tyer-PYET nye mo-GU…
Терпеть не могу…

> **Rock 'n' roll**
> *rok-n-roll*
> Рок-н-ролл

DIRTY MARTINI

Pregame for the concert with a classic. It will set you up to dance the night away.

GET THESE:

2½ ounces vodka
½ ounce dry vermouth
¼ to ½ ounce olive juice
3 martini olives, for garnish

DO THIS:

Put the first 3 ingredients in a shaker with ice. Shake until your arms ache and strain into a martini glass. Pierce the olives onto a cocktail pick and place them inside the martini glass. Drink enough of these so you don't feel silly dancing like a lunatic.

There are some decent bands in Russia that play traditional rock. Two of the most famous are Чиж & Co (*Chizh & Co*) and Наутилус Помпилиус (*Nautilus Pompilius*), which wrote the hit song Гуд-бай Америка ("Good-bye, America"), among other rock classics.

Pop
pop-SA
Попса

Unfortunately, boy bands have been pretty popular in Russia, including such nauseating acts as Руки вверх (*Ruki vverkh*) and Иванушки Интернэшнл (*Ivanushki International*). And then there was the teen lesbo duo T.A.T.U. All in all, it's a pretty depressing scene. There are some halfway decent alternative pop groups, though, including Земфира (*Zemfira*), Ночные снайперы (*Nochnie sniperi*), Мумий Тролль (*Mummy Troll*), and Сплин (*Spleen*). There are also some good Ukrainian alterno-pop groups that have had some crossover success in Russia, such as Воплі Відоплясова (*Vopli Vidoplyasova*) and Океан Ельзи (*Okean Elzi*), whose music is featured on the soundtrack to *Brat 2*, truly one of the greatest compilation albums to come out of Russia in the last ten years. The Ukrainian drag act Верка Сердючка (*Verka Serduchka*) is entertaining in small doses. And then there's the Ukrainian threesome Via Gra. I think the name says it all.

Alternative

al-tyer-na-TI-va
Альтернатива

Probably the best Russian rock-alternative groups around these days are Tequila Jazz, Аукцыон (*Auktsyon*), the Belarusian band Ляпис Трубецкой (*Lyapis Trubetskoi*), and Найк Борзов (*Naik Borzov*), who does something like acoustic-alternative.

Heavy metal

KHE-vi-ME-tal
Хэви-метал

Not really my thing, but there are a few well-known Russian metal bands out there, including Ария (*Aria*), Легион (*Legion*), Эпидемия (*Epidemia*), and Catharsis. Heavy metal is sometimes also called Мясо (*MYA-so*), which literally means "meat."

Punk rock

pank-rok
Панк-рок

There are actually some pretty good punk bands in Russia. Probably the best known is Гражданская оборона (*Grazhdanskaya oborona*). Other fairly accomplished groups are Тараканы (*Tarakani*), Наив (*Naïve*), and perhaps Король и Шут (*Korol i Shut*).

Ska

Ска

Me? I like ska. And if you're anything like me, you'll definitely want to check out the band Ленинград (*Leningrad*): They are best—and the most obscene—around. Hey, anyone who writes a song called Полный пиздец (*Polnii pidyetz*), or "Totally Fucked," gets a thumbs up from me. Also worth checking out is their equally rockin'—if somewhat less raunchy—spinoff band, Spitfire.

Reggae

Реггей/Регги

Russian reggae is pretty hit or miss. There are actually a surprisingly large number of reggae bands, but probably the most widely known are 5'nizza (*Pyatnitsa*), Республика Jah (*Respublika Jah*), K.O.T., and Bro Sound.

CHASTUSHKI)))

CHAS-TUSH-KI
ЧАСТУШКИ

Chastushki are sort of like Russian limericks set to music, usually accompanied by an accordion and sung off key either by a drunken, sweaty *muzhik* or a *baba* with a whiney voice trying to sound folksy. But on the upside, they're usually pretty funny, at least if you've had a few drinks. Here are a few examples. Note that these translations are more artistic than literal.

Я с милёнком целовалась,
Целовалась горячо.
Я ещё бы целовалась,
Да болит влагалищо.

ya s mi-LYON-kom tse-lo-VA-las,
tse-lo-VA-las go-rya-CHO.
ya ye-SCHO bi tse-lo-VA-las,
da bo-LIT vla-GA-li-scho.

> I and my honey did some kissing,
>
> We are hot and heavy flirts.
>
> I would like to kiss him more,
>
> But my vagina already hurts.

Отведу мою милашку
К зелёному дубу.
Пусть её ебёт медведь,
Я больше не буду.

ot-vye-DU mo-YU mi-LASH-ku
k zye-LYO-no-mu DU-bu.
pust ye-YO ye-BYOT myed-VYED,
ya BOL-she nye BU-du.

> I'm gonna take my girl
>
> Away to the green oak woods.
>
> Let some bear fuck her there,
>
> I've had enough of her of goods.

Шёл я лесом, видел беса,
Бес картошечку варил.
Котелок на хуй повесил,
А из жопы дым валил.

shol ya LYE-som, VI-dyel BYE-sa,
byes kar-TO-shech-ku va-RIL.
ko-tye-LOK na khui po-VYE-sil,
a iz ZHO-pi dim va-LIL.

> In the forest I saw a devil,
>
> He was boiling potatoes fast.
>
> He hung a kettle on his dick,
>
> And smoke came out his ass.

Меня в армию призвали,
Я пришел в военкомат.
Грудь широка, руки белы,
Только хуй коротковат.

me-NYA v AR-mi-yu priz-VA-li,
ya pri-SHOL v vo-yen-ko-MAT.
grud shi-ro-KA, RU-ki bye-LI,
TOL-ko khui ko-rot-ko-VAT.

> I was drafted to the army,
>
> So I went to the military hall.
>
> My chest is wide, my hands are white,
>
> Only my dick is a bit too small.

В гости я пришел к японке, *v GOS-ti ya pri-SHOL k ya-PON-kye*
Стан обнять пытался тонкий. *stan ob-NYAT pi-TAL-sya TON-kii*
-Нет! -кричит она. -Сперва *—nyet!—kri-CHIT o-NA. —SPYER-va*
Отдавайте острова. *ot-da-VAI-tye os-tro-VA.*

I went to visit a Japanese dame
I tried to hug her waist so lean.
"No!" she began to me exclaim,
"First give us back Sakhalin."

Пароход плывет по Волге, *pa-ro-KHOD pli-VYOT po VOL-gye*
Небо голубеется. *NYE-bo go-lu-BYE-ye-tsa*
Девки едут без билета - *DYEV-ki YE-dut byez bi-LYE-ta*
На пизду надеются. *na piz-DU na-DYE-yu-tsa.*

A steamer sails along the Volga
As the sky is shining blue.
Gals have boarded without tickets
They plan on paying with a screw.

Rap/Hip-hop
rep/khip-KHOP
Рэп/Хип-хоп

Wigga takes on a whole new meaning in Russia and something about it just ain't right. Some well-known rap/hip-hop bands (and I use that term loosely) in Russia include Мальчишник (*Malchishnik*), Отпетые мошенники (*Otpyetiye moshenniki*), Кирпичи (*Kirpichi*), Дельфин (*Delfin*), and Серёга (*Seryoga*) whose ridiculous song Чёрный бумер (*Chornii Bumer*), or "Black Beemer," got WAY too much airtime. For some reason, hip-hop is really popular in Ukraine with such notable, if absurdly white, acts as ТНМК (*TNMK*) and Грин грей (*Green Gray*).

Indie
IN-di-rok
Инди-рок

There are a few Indie groups around, including Vertigo.

Lounge music
launzh
Лаунж

Probably the best-known lounge act these days is Нож для Фрау Мюллер (*Nozh dlya Frau Muller*) which plays a kind of electro-lounge.

TECHNO

TYEKH-NO

ТЕХНО

I don't know, other than maybe Thaivox, I just can't get into techno crap. But if trance beats are your thing, then here are some styles. Frankly, I can't even tell the difference between them.

Trip Hop	*trip-khop*	Трип-хоп
Drum n Bass	*dram-n-beis*	Драм-н-бейс
Electro-House	*e-LYEK-tro-khaus*	Электро-хау
Hi-NRG	*khai-E-ner-ji*	Хай-Энерджи
Industrial	*in-dus-tri-AL-na-ya*	Индустриальная

Funk

fank

Фанк

One of the best Russian contemporary bands around is the funkadelic Детский Панадол (*Dyetsky Panadol*). It's also one of the funniest names of a band I've heard in a while.

Jazz

jaz

Джаз

There are actually a number of good jazz clubs around Moscow, if the music doesn't bore you to death before you even have time to down your first round.

"Author music"

AV-tor-ska-ya MU-zi-ka

Авторская музыка

This term usually refers to the so-called барды (*BAR-di*) of the Russian musical tradition. It sometimes sounds something like folk rock, is often acoustic, and the main criterion is that the singer write his own lyrics. It's fairly popular in Russia, and two of the most famous examples are Владимир Высоцкий (*Vladimir Vysotsky*) and Булат Окуджава (*Bulat Okudzhava*). Both are dead but still listened to a lot more often than many living singers.

Shanson
Шансон

If you make a habit of taking cabs in Russia, likely you'll become well acquainted with *Shanson*. This was originally the music of criminals and wannabe thugs, but now it's all over the place. A good example of this genre is the late Михаил Круг (*Mikhail Krug*) and his strangely catchy ballad Владимирский централ (*Vladimirskii Tsentral*). This music is also sometimes referred to as Блатная музыка (*blat-NA-ya MU-zi-ka*), a term that betrays its prison camp origins.

Russian stage music
ro-SSII-ska-ya es-TRA-da
Российская эстрада

Middle-aged Russians love this stuff, and you'll be lucky if you can escape a trip to Russia without being subjected to the musical stylings of pop diva Алла Борисовна Пугачёва (*Alla Borisovna Pugachova*), Russia's answer to Barbra Streisand, and her former husband, the freakishly flamboyant Филипп Киркоров (*Filipp Kirkorov*). On the other hand, the more hard-rockin' act Любэ (*Lyube*) isn't half bad if you're into civilians dressing up in military uniform and singing the praises of the armed forces.

R&B
air-en-bi
Айренби

Country
KAN-tri
Кантри

Blues
blyuz
Блюз

Disco
DIS-ko
Диско

Acoustic
a-KUS-ti-ka
Акустика

Electronic music
e-lyek-TRO-na-ya MU-zi-ka
Электронная музыка

·····In the band
v BEN-dye
В бэнде

That's really a cool band!
*E-to KLASS_nii **bend**!*
Это классный **бэнд**!

They're an awesome group!
*o-NI o-bal-DYE-nna-ya **GRU-ppa**!*
Они обалденная **группа**!

I really like Leningrad's new album.
*mnye O-chen NRA-vi-tsya NO-vii **al-BOM** lye-nin-GRA-da.*
Мне очень нравится новый **альбом** Ленинграда.

I hear DDT is going on tour this summer.
*ya SLI-shal, chto DDT LYE-tom YE-dut na **ga-STRO-li**.*
Я слышал, что ДДТ летом приедут на **гастроли**.

Zemfira's new song is a real hit.
*NO-va-ya PYES-nya zem-FI-ri—na-sto-YA-schii **khit**.*
Новая песня Земфиры—настоящий **хит**.

That stupid song is just pop crap.
*E-ta du-RATS-ka-ya PYES-nya SLISH-kom **pop-SO-va-ya**.*
Эта дурацкая песня слишком **попсовая**.

I dig the rhythm of reggae.
*ya ta-SCHUS ot **RIT-ma** RE-ggi.*
Я тащусь от **ритма** регги.

I went to an amazing concert last night.
*ya vchye-RA kho-DIL na o-fi-GYE-nnii **kon-TSERT**.*
Я вчера ходил на офигенный **концерт**.

My friend works as a DJ at radio station.
*moi drug ra-BO-ta-yet **di-je-yem** na ra-di-o-STAN-tsii.*
Мой друг работает ди-**джеем** на радиостанции.

Are all disks in Russia really pirated?
*nye-u-ZHE-li vsye DIS-ki v ro-SSII **pi-RAT-ski-ye**?*
Неужели все диски в России **пиратские**?
Батарейки сели в моём **плеере**.

Do you know where I can see some good break dancing?
*ti nye ZNA-yesh gdye MOZN-no po-smo-TRYET kho-RO-shii **breik-dens**?*
Ты не знаешь где можно посмотреть хороший **брейк-дэнс**?

I'm a big fan of Tsoi.
*ya bol-ZHOI **po-KLO-nnik** TSO-ya.*
Я большой **поклонник** Цоя.

That pop star always gives autographs to his fans.
*E-ta **pop-zvyez-DA** vsyeg-DA da-YOT svo-IM **fa-NAT-kam** av-TO-gra-fi.*
Эта **поп-звезда** всегда даёт своим **фанаткам** автографы.

I'm a total music freak!
*ya vo-ob-SCHE **mye-lo-MAN**!*
Я вообще **меломан**!

Prerecorded music (for singers to essentially perform karaoke style on stage)
mi-nu-SOV-ka
Минусовка

Recorded song (used for pop stars to lip-synch on stage)
fa-NYE-ra
Фанера

Guitar amp
pri-MOCH-ka
Примочка

Rehearsal (slang)
RYE-pa
Репа
This is short for репетиция (*rye-pye-TI-tsi-ya*)

·····The Legends of Leningrad
lye-GYEN-di lye-nin-GRA-da
Легенды Ленинграда

The rock scene in Russia really took off in the late '70s/early '80s just before and during the glasnost era. Before that, there was only the "official" Soviet music scene, which was pretty awful, and a local underground that mainly comprised the aforementioned bards like Vysotsky and Okudzhava. There were the be-boppin' стиляги (*stilyagi*) in the '50s and various counterculture movements throughout the '60s and '70s, but they were listening mainly to Western records smuggled into the country and sold on the black market. When homegrown Russian rock finally took off, it was in the Leningrad Rock Club, and those early years spawned the original Russian Monsters of Rock.

Akvarium
Аквариум

This band really annoys the hell out of me. Some of their early stuff isn't half bad, but ultimately their legendary lead singer Борис Гребенщиков (*Boris Grebenschikov*), often referred to simply as БГ (*BG*), developed an obsessive interest in Buddhism and eastern mysticism and came to consider himself a deep intellectual type. The result was less rock and more esoteric, artsy themes accompanied by melodies influenced by reggae, jazz, and folk music. Not surprisingly, it sucks. But, hey, if you're an aging hippie who, despite falling victim to male-pattern baldness still sports a ponytail, you might just get into these guys.

Alisa
Алиса

Alisa used to rock hard, and they often performed their concerts clad in tight black denim and leather, black nail polish, and Kiss-like stage makeup. Unfortunately, they started getting old and flabby, and for a while turned to more jazz- and folk-inspired music. Their newer stuff is a little more hard rockin' and isn't really that bad despite the blatant nationalist themes, but it's just kind of depressing to watch punks get old. I feel the same sense of despair every time I see an interview with John Lydon.

Kino
Кино

The lead singer of Kino was Виктор Цой (*Viktor Tsoi*), whose angst-filled lyrics and untimely death in a car accident in 1990 has made him into a kind of Russian Kurt Cobain. His cult status in Russia has led to creation of the Tsoi memorial wall just off Arbat in Moscow where you can almost always catch a few local stoners drinking port wine and leaving behind cigarettes as sacrificial offerings to their god, and apparently there are current plans to erect some sort of monument in his honor in St. Petersburg. In fact, Tsoi is still so admired that in 2000 some of the hottest rock and pop artists in Russia released a rockin' tribute album called Кинопробы *(Kinoproby)* on which they covered some of Kino's greatest hits. In addition to his music, Tsoi is also sometimes remembered for his starring role in the cult classic Игла (*Igla*), or *The Needle*. I have to admit that I have a soft spot for him, but then I am prone to agonizing bouts of crippling depression.

DDT
ДДТ

Originally from the Uralic backwater of Ufa, DDT managed to skyrocket to international acclaim though hard work, gritty lyrics, and a whole lotta soul. Now, they may be considered totally old school by some, but I personally think that Юрий Шевчук (*Yuri Shevchuk*) is still one of the baddest mofos around. He's doing a lot of solo work these days, and most of his new stuff is both cynical and political without being clichéd. If you ask me, that just never goes out of style.

⋯⋯PC speak
PC sleng
PC сленг

There's a good reason that every Russian living in the U.S. seems to work as a computer programmer. Russians kick ass at this shit, and they are known to be some of the most skilled hackers around. You know that last virus your computer caught? Likely it was created by some Russian teenager just goofing around after class. So why can't they come up with their own words for PC speak?

My **operating system** fucking crashed again.
*mo-YA **o-pye-ra-TSON-ka** o-PYAT piz-DOI na-KRI-las.*
Моя **операционка** опять пиздой накрылась.

My computer is infected with a **virus**.
*moi kom-PYU-ter za-RA-zhen **VI-ru-som**.*
Мой компьютер заражен **вирусом**.

I don't know how **to use** a Mac.
ya nye u-MYE-yu
***YU-zat** mak.*
Я не умею
юзать Мак.
From the English verb
"to use."

I'll **photocopy** it for
you.
ya te-BYE ot-KSYER-
yu.
Я **тебе отксерю**.
From the brand name
Xerox.

I'll **scan** it for you.
*ya te-BYE **ot-ska-NI-ru-yu**.*
Я тебе **отсканирую**.
From the English verb "to scan."

You can **fax** it to him.
*Mo-zhesh ye-MU **po-SLAT po FAK-su**.*
Можешь ему **послать по факсу**.

For some reason I can't **attach** this **file**.
*CHTO-to nye mo-GU **pri-a-TTA-chat** E-tot **fail**.*
Что-то не могу **приаттачать** этот **файл**.
Both from English words: "attach" and "file."

If you **download** the program, I can **install** it for
you.
*YES-li **ska-CHA-yesh** E-tu pro-GRA-mmu, ya po-mo-*
*GU te-BYE **u-sta-no-VIT**.*
Если **скачаешь** эту программу, я помогу тебе
установить.

Also...

Cell (phone)
mo-BIL-ka
Мобилка

SMS
es-em-ES-ka
СМС-ка

To text
tyek-sto-VAT
Текстовать

•••••The World Wide Web
myezh-du-na-ROD-na-ya syet
Международная сеть

As the internet became increasingly popular in Russia, there was an explosion in Russian-language websites offering everything from explicit sites to satisfy your porn addiction to online term papers you can download and plagiarize, to pirated films where for a small "membership fee" you can see the next Hollywood blockbuster even before Hollywood does, and all from the comfort of your lousy windowless cubicle. As with music, the vast majority of internet terms are taken directly from English.

I met my fiancée online.
*ya po-zna-KO-mil-sya so svo-YEI nye-VYES-toi v **on-lAiN-ye**.*
Я познакомился со своей невестой в **онлайне**.

I really liked her profile.
*mnye O-chen po-NYA-vil-sya ye-YO **PRO-fil**.*
Мне очень понравился её **профиль**.

I posted on a forum.
ya za-po-STIL-sya na FO-ru-mye.
Я запостился на форуме.

We got to know each better in a chat room.
*mi po-zna-KO-mi-lis po-BLI-zhe SI-dya v **CHA-tye**.*
Мы познакомились поближе сидя в **чате**.

She sent me a PM.
o-NA na-pi-SA-la mnye v LICH-ku.
Она написала мне в **личку**.

My posts were so stupid that the moderator banned me.
o-I pos-TI BI-li na-STOL-ko du-TATS-ki-ye, chto mo-de-RA-tor me-NYA za-ba-NIL.
Мои посты были настолько дурацкие, что модератор меня **забанил**.

I flamed some idiot and got banned.
ya SDYE-lal ka-KO-mu-to i-di-O-tu fleim i po-lu-CHIL ban.
Я сделал какому-то идиоту **флейм** и получил **бан**.

Now the fucking site won't accept my log-in and password.
tye-PYER E-tot YO-ba-nnii sait nye pri-ni-MA-yet mo-YO I-mya POL-zo-va-tye-lya i pa-ROL.
Теперь этот ёбаный **сайт** не принимает моё **имя пользователя и пароль**.

So later, we chatted on ICQ.
TAK chto, po-TOM mi ob-SCHA-lis v AS-kye.
Так что, потом мы общались **в аське**.

We still haven't met IRL.
mi ye-SCHO nye VSTRYE-ti-lis v re-A-lye.
Мы ещё не встретились **в реале**.

She has sent me some pics by e-mail.
o-NA mnye FOT-ki SKI-nula po MI-lu.
Она мне фотки скинула **по мылу**.

If NE1 doubts our love, they should see all the emojis we use.
YES-li kto-nit som-nye-VA-ye-tsya v NA-shei lyub-VI, o-NI bi u-VI-dye-li ka-KI-ye mi is-POL-zu-yem SMAI-li-ki.
Если **кто-нить** сомневается в нашей любви, они бы увидели какие мы используем **смайлики**.

I just **registered** on odnoklassniki.ru.

*ya TOL-ko chto **za-rye-gi-STRI-ro-val-sya** na od-no-KLASS-ni-kakh TOCH-ka ru.*

Я только что **зарегистрировался** на одноклассники.ru.

Odnoklassniki is one of the most popular Russian social networking sites.

You can read all about it on my **blog**.

*MOZH-no o-bo VSYOM pro-chi-TAT na mo-YOM **BLO-gye**.*

Можно обо всём прочитать на моём **блоге**.

And not surprisingly, a blogger is called a блоггер (*BLO-gger*).

I spend a lot of time on the **web**.

ya MNO-go VRYE-mye-ni pro-vo-ZHU v sye-TI.

Я много времени провожу в **сети**.

My **username** is...

*moi **nik**...*

Мой **ник**...

I also have my own **page** on **Live Journal**.

*u me-NYA TO-zhe yest svo-YA **stra-NI-tsa na zhi-VOM zhur-NA-lye**.*

У меня тоже есть своя **страница на Живом журнале**.

The blogging site Live Journal is pretty popular in Russia and is often referred to simply as ЖЖ (*ZhZh*).

I'll send you the link to my **web page**.

*ya te-BYE po-SHLU SSIL-ku na mo-YU **veb-stra-NI-tsu**.*

Я тебе пошлю ссылку на мою **веб-страницу**.

Do you have an **e-mail address**?

*u te-BYA YEST **A-dryes e-lyek-TRO-nnoi POCH-ti**?*

У тебя есть **адрес электронной почты**?

My **e-mail** is...

*moi **e-meil**...*

Мой **е-мэйл**...

Note that the symbol @ used in e-mail addresses is pronounced as собачка (*so-BACH-ka*).

I am so sick of **spam**.

*mnye tak na-do-YEL **spam**.*

Мне так надоел **спам**.

·····Netspeak
ya-ZIK pa-DON-kov
Язык падонков

The Russian internet has a language all its own, and it's called язык падонков (*yazik padonkov*), which literally translates to something along the lines of "scumbag language," and this name, like most of the language itself, is sometimes spelled in various creative ways, such as йазыг падонкафф (*iazig padonkaff*). There are two main sources for this slang: Russified English and phonetically spelled Russian. Because of this, it can be a little tricky to read at first, but you'll get used to it after a while. Some of the most common *padonkov* terms are:

Hi!
prye-VYED!
Превед!
From the Russian привет.

Hey there, bear!
prye-VYED, myed-VYED!
Превед, медвед!
This is actually a famous and widely quoted line from a comic strip.

Sorry for the OT.
*SO-rri za **off-top**.*
Сорри за **оффтоп**.

Misc.
flud
Флуд
Some forums have a section dedicated to discussion of all kinds of miscellaneous crap. That section is called the флуд (*flud*), or the флудилка (*flu-DIL-ka*).

Y'all have posted a lot of crap here!
*nu i **na-flu-DI-li** tut!*
Ну и **нафлудили** тут!
This is usually the criticism when people have posted a bunch of random stuff outside the designated area.

Pet name for Google

GO-sha

Гоша

Pet name for Yandex (the largest Russian Web portal and search engine)

YA-sha

Яша

ROFL!

a-ba-SSA-ka!

Абассака!

Fucking kewl!

pyes-DA-to!

Песдато!

From пиздато.

A+

pyat BA-llov

5 баллов

This is a reference to the five-point Russian grading system.

FO (Fuck off)

u-BYEI se-BYA ap-STYE-nu

Убей себя апстену

From убей себя об стену, or "kill yourself against a wall."

That's so cool, I'll take two

a-khu-YET, DAI-tye dvye

Ахуеть, дайте две

GR8

ATS-tskii

Аццкий

From адский.

(You have my) respect!

rye-SPYEKT!

Респект!

Funny as Hell

a-fi-GYEN-ski

Афигенски

So Fucking Stupid

f TOP-ku

Ф топку

Die in a Fire
VI-pyei IA-du
Выпей йаду
From выпей яду, or "drink poison."

Beautiful Beyond Belief
gla-MUR-nyen-ko
Гламурненько

You the man!
za-CHOT!
Зачот!

Don't Give a Fuck
i nii-PYOT
И ниипёт

2 Kewl
ni-pa-DYE-tski
Нипадецки
From не по детски.

2 Drunk 2 Type
fgav-NO
Фгавно
From в гавно.

LMAO
pats-to-LOM
Пацтолом
From под столом.

Beyach
STSU-ko
Сцуко
From сука.

OMFG!
u-zho-SNAKH
Ужоснах

Comments, please
KO-mmyen-ti, pliz
Комменты, плиз

First! (as in "First poster to comment on a thread")
PYER-vii-nakh!
Первыйнах!

You crack me up
rzhu-ni-ma-GU
Ржунимагу
From ржу–не могу.

Old Freaking News
ba-YAN
Баян

A post of some kind of creative value
kri-a-TIFF
Криатифф
From "creative."

Author
aff-TAR
Аффтар
Refers to an internet writer, either a poster on a forum or a blogger. From the Russian word автор.

The author is on fire!
aff-TAR zhzhot
Аффтар жжот
From автор зажигает.

The author rules!
aff-TAR rulz!
Аффтар рулз!
From the English word "rules."

We rule!
mi RU-lim!
Мы рулим!
Also from "to rule."

·····LOL
r-ZHA-ka
Ржака

Like English internet language, *yazik padonkov* makes frequent use of abbreviations and acronyms.

ZFB
ЗФБ

This stands for Зи Факинг Бэст, a transliteration of English "the fucking best."

ИМХО

This is a direct transliteration from the English "IMHO."

KG/AM
КГ/АМ

This stands for креатиф гавно, афтар мудак, translated as "the post is shit and the author is an ass."

Ы

Similar to LOL. It doesn't really stand for anything, though. I guess it just looks like laughing in some way.

АЖ/КЗ
Azh/KZ

This stands for аффтар жжот, креатифф зачотный, translated as something like "the author is on fire, and the post rocks."

PPKS
ППКС

Stands for подпишусь под каждым словом, the equivalent of the English ITA.

ЗЫ

If you turn on the Russian keyboard and hit the keys that correspond to the Latin letters PS, this is what you get. Hence, it means "PS."

CHAPTER 8

SPORTY RUSSIAN

SPOR-TIV-NII RU-SSKII
Спортивный русский

Ah, sports. The Soviet Union was legendary for them and for all the gold medals Soviet athletes won in the Olympics. Although those glory days may be fading into the past, sports are still a pretty big deal in Russia, especially soccer and hockey, even though the best of the players have fled abroad for greater fame, more lucrative endorsements, and far better training facilities. Sports in Russia are reputed to be very closely connected to organized crime—no surprise, really: Where there is money to be made, there are always people looking for their cut.

·····I'm into sports

ya u-vlye-KA-yus SPOR-tom
Я увлекаюсь спортом

Who do you root for—Dinamo or Spartak?
za ko-VO ti bo-LYE-yesh—za di-NA-mo ili spar-TAK?
За кого ты **болеешь**—за Динамо или Спартак?

I'm rooting for Russia.
ya bo-LYE-yu za ro-SSI-yu.
Я болею за Россию.

🍸 THE PENALTY SHOT

Did you body check the other player on the ice? Good job. Oh wait, did you get caught by the ref? That's a penalty shot. Drink!

GET THESE:

    1 ounce vodka
    1 ounce pickle juice
    pickle slice, for garnish
    habanero pepper, for garnish (optional)

DO THIS:

Put the liquid ingredients in a cocktail shaker with ice and shake until well chilled. Strain into a shot glass and garnish with a pickle slice. Change the garnish to a pickled habanero pepper if the other team scores. That'll teach you to get caught.

Who's the **favorite**?
*kto **fa-vo-RIT**?*
Кто **фаворит**?

I always pull for the **underdog**.
*ya vsyeg-DA bo-LYE-yu za **an-dyer-DOG***.
Я всегда болею за **андердог**.

Let's grab a beer at **halftime**.
*da-VAI za PI-vom vo VRYE-mya **PA-uzi***.
Давай за пивом во время **паузы**.

What **half** is it now?
*ka-KOI sei-CHAS **taim**?*
Какой сейчас **тайм**?

The **opposing team** sucks balls.
***so-PYER-ni-ki**—pi-de-RA-si!*
Соперники—пидарасы!

We got beat in **overtime**.
*nas ob-i-GRA-li v **do-pol-NI-tyel-no-ye VRYE-mya***.
Нас обыграли в **дополнительное время**.

Real **fans** don't like **glory hunters**.
*na-sto-YA-shi-ye **bo-LYEL-schi-ki** nye LYU-byat **kuz-mi-CHO-va***.
Настоящие **болельщики** не любят **Кузьмичёва**.

Do you think he dopes?
kak ti DU-ma-yesh, on pri-ni-MA-yet DO-ping?
Как ты думаешь, он **принимает допинг**?

He's open!
on ot-KRIT!
Он открыт!

The Olympic Games
o-lim-PIIS-ki-ye I-gri
Олимпийские игры

What are Russia's chances at the Olympics this year?
ka-KI-ye u ro-SSII SHAN-si na o-lim-pi-A-dye v E-tom go-DU?
Какие у России шансы на **Олимпиаде** в этом году?

Do you think Russia will win any gold medals?
kak ti DU-ma-yesh, vi-i-GRA-yet li ro-SSI-ya zo-lo-TI-ye mye-DA-li?
Как ты думаешь, выиграет ли Россия **золотые медали**?

Honored Master of Sports
za-SLU-zhe-nii MAS-ter SPOR-ta ro-SSII
Заслуженный мастер спорта России
This is the title given to Russian most accomplished athletes, similar to a Hall of Famer.

·····The major sports
GLAV-ni-ye VI-di SPOR-ta
Главные виды спорта

Soccer
fut-BOL
Футбол
Like most of the world, Russians call soccer "football."
If you want talk about what Americans call football, it is американский футбол (*a-me-ri-KAN-skii fut-BOL*), or American football.

Goalie
vra-TAR
Вратарь

MARTIAL ARTS)))

BO-YE-VI-YE IS-KU-SSTVA
БОЕВЫЕ ИСКУССТВА

Judo	jyu-DO	Дзюдо
Karate	ka-ra-TE	Каратэ
Aikido	ai-ki-DO	Айкидо
Jujitsu	ji-u-JIT-su	Джиу-джитсу
Tai kwon do	tae--kvon-DO	Таэквон-до

Fullback
za-SCHIT-nik
Защитник

Halfback
po-lu-za-SCHIT-nik
Полузащитник

Uh-oh, the ref is pulling out the yellow card.
*O-pa! KA-zhe-tsya RYE-fe-ri prye-dya-VLYA-yet **gor-CHICH-nik**.*
Опа! Кажется рефери предъявляет **горчичник**.

That dipshit just kicked the ball into his own post!
*E-tot loch TOL-ko chto za-BRO-sil myach v svo-I **vo-RO-ta**!*
Этот лох только что забросил мяч в свои **ворота**!

Holy shit! He totally scored a hat trick!
*yob! On vo-ob-SCHE o-FOR-mil **khet-trik**!*
Ёб! Он вообще оформил **хет-трик**!

Goooooooaaaaaaal!
goooooooool!
Гоооооооол!

Please, oh lord, let us win the penalty shootout.
*GOS-po-di, dai nam VI-i-grat **SYE-ri-yu pye-NAL-ti***.
Господи, дай нам выиграть **серию пенальти**.

Fuck! Another draw!
*blyad, o-PYAT **ni-CHYA**!*
Блядь, опять **ничья**!

World Championship of Soccer
chem-pi-o-NAT MI-ra po fut-BOL-u
Чемпионат мира по футболу
Usually abbreviated as ЧМ (*ChM*).

The 4 B's
che-TI-re be
4Б
This stands for the four B's of Russian soccer: Бил, Бью, Буду Бить ("I've scored, I score, I will score"). This was the motto of the famous Russian footballer Aleksandr Kerzhakov.

Who do you think will win the **UEFA Cup** this year?
*kak ti DU-ma-yesh, kto vi-i-GRA-yet **KU-bok u-ef-a** v E-tom go-DU?*
Как ты думаешь, кто выиграет **Кубок УЕФА** в этом году?

Hockey
kho-KKYEI
Хоккей

Stanley Cup
KU-bok STYE-nli
Кубок Стэнли

Did you see how he slammed that **puck** in the net?
*ti VI-dyel, kak on za-BRO-sil **SHAI-bu** v SYET-ku?*
Ты видел, как он забросил **шайбу** в сетку?

Hey, he should get a **penalty shot** for that!
*ei, on DOL-zhen za E-to po-lu-CHIT **BU-llit**!*
Эй, он должен за это получить **буллит**!

What's the penalty for **boarding**?
*ka-KOI shtraf na **tol-CHOK na bort**?*
Какой штраф на **толчок на борт**?

Tennis
TYE-nnis
Теннис

Wimbledon Championships
u-im-bl-DON-skii tur-NIR
Уимблдонский турнир

Nice **backhand**!
*KLASS-nii **u-DAR SLYE-va**!*
Классный **удар слева**!

Anna Kournikova looks smokin' in her tennis whites.
A-nna KUR-ni-ko-va o-fi-GYE-nno VI-glya-dit v svo-YOM TYE-nnis-nom ko-STYU-mye.
Анна Курникова офигенно выглядит в своём **теннисном костюме**.

Figure skating
fi-GUR-no-ye ka-TA-ni-ye
Фигурное катание

That was an amazing double axel!
E-to bil o-bal-DYE-nii dvoi-NOI AK-syel!
Это был обалденный **двойной аксель**!

The Russian judges always cheat.
RU-sski-ye SU-dyi vsyeg-DA much-LYU-yut.
Русские **судьи** всегда мухлюют.

Are all male figure skaters gay?
RAZ-vye vsye muzh-SKI-ye fi-gu-RIS-ti go-lu-BI-ye?
Разве все мужские **фигуристы** голубые?

Gymnastics
gim-NAS-ti-ka
Гимнастика

I bet that gymnast would be wild in bed!
na-vyer-nya-KA E-ta gim-NAST-ka bye-ZUM-na v po-STYE-li!
Наверняка эта **гимнастка** безумна в постели!

The chicks always blow it on the **balance beam**.
*DYEV-ki vsyeg-DA ob-LA-mi-va-yu-tsya na **bryev-NYE***.
Девки всегда обламываются на **бревне**.

The **uneven bars** are the shit!
***raz-no-vi-SO-ki-ye BRU-sya**—SA-ma-ya kru-tiz-NA!*
Разновысокие брусья—самая крутизна!

Boxing
boks
Бокс

What a knockout! That hadda hurt!
ka-KOI nok-A-ut! E-to na-VYER-no-ye BOL-no!
Какой нокаут! Это наверное больно!

Weightlifting
tya-ZHO-la-ya at-LYE-ti-ka
Тяжёлая атлетика

Weightlifter
shtan-GIST
Штангист

Sure, **steroids** make you strong, but they also make you sterile.
*ko-NYECH-no **stye-RO-i-d**i DYE-la-yut te-BYA SIL-nim, no ye-SCHO DYE-la-yut te-BYA byes-PLOD-nim.*
Конечно **стероиды** делают тебя сильным, но ещё делают тебя бесплодным.

Skiing
ka-TA-ni-ye na LI-zhakh
Катание на лыжах

I hate cross-country, but I love **downhill skiing**.
*ya nye-na-VI-zhu **LIZH-ni-ye GON-ki**, no lyu-BLYU **GOR-ni-ye LI-zhi**.*
Я ненавижу **лыжные гонки**, но люблю **горные лыжи**.

Free-style skiing (фристайл) is pronounced like in the English (*fri-STAIL*).

·····Other kinds of sports

dru-GI-ye VI-di SPOR-ta

Другие виды спорта

Track and field
LYOG-ka-ya at-LYE-ti-ka

Лёгкая атлетика

> **That runner is a doper.**
> *E-tot **bye**-GUN — KHI-mik.*
> Этот **бегун** — химик.

Water sports
VOD-ni-ye VI-di SPOR-ta

Водные виды спорта

Swimming
PLA-va-ni-ye

Плавание

Note that there are two basic verbs meaning "to swim": плавать (*PLA-vat*) refers to something like swimming laps, whereas купаться (*ku-PA-tsya*) is more like going for a dip/goofing around in the water.

Surfing
SYOR-fing

Сёрфинг

> **Man, the waves are really weak here.**
> *blin, VOL-ni tut khye-RO-vi-ye.*
> Блин, волны тут херовые.

Fishing
ri-BAL-ka

Рыбалка

> **Do you know where I could do some fishing?**
> *ti nye ZNA-yesh, gdye tut MOZH-no po-ri-BA-chit?*
> Ты не знаешь, где тут можно порыбачить?

Extreme sports
ek-STRIM sport

Экстрим спорт

> #### Skateboarding
> *skeit-BOR-ding*
> Скейтбординг
> Sometimes just called скейт (*skeit*).

That was one awesome skate ramp!
*E-tot **drop** bil SU-pyer-skii!*
Этот **дроп** был суперский!

Snowboarding
sno-u-BOR-ding
Сноубординг

Skydiving
prizh-kl s pa-ra-SHU-tom
Прыжки с парашютом

Rock climbing
ska-lo-LA-za-ni-ye
Скалолазание

Auto racing
av-to-GON-ki
Автогонки

Drag racing
drag REI-sing
Драг рейсинг

·····Exercise
u-prazh-NYE-ni-ye
Упражнение

I do...
ya za-ni-MA-yus...
Я занимаюсь...
Remember, this verb takes the instrumental case.

yoga.
YO-goi.
йогой.

aerobics.
ae-RO-bi-koi.
аэробикой.

bodybuilding.
bo-di-BIL-din-gom.
бодибилдингом.

powerlifting.
po-uer-LIF-tin-gom.
пауэрлифтингом.

DANCING)))

TAN-TSI

ТАНЦЫ

Ballroom dancing	*BAL-ni-ye TAN-tsi*	Бальные танцы
Ballet	*ba-LYET*	Балет
Folk dancing	*na-ROD-ni-ye TAN-tsi*	Народные танцы
Salsa	*SAL-sa*	Сальса
Belly dancing	*TA-nyets zh*	*i-vo-TA* Танец живота
Tango	*TAN-go*	Танго
Hip-hop	*khip KHOP*	Хип-хоп
Swing	*sving*	Свинг

dance.

TAN-tsa-mi.

танцами.

Where can I do some pull-ups?

gdye tut MOZH-no DYE-lat pod-TYA-gi-va-ni-ye?

Где тут можно делать подтягивание?

Do you know a good gym?

*ti nye ZNA-yesh kho-RO-shii **trye-ni-RO-voch-nii zal**?*

Ты не знаешь хороший **тренировочный зал**?

Where can I work out?

*gdye MOZH-no **po-trye-ni-ro-VA-tsya**?*

Где можно **потренироваться**?

Do a lot of people jog in Russia?

*MNO-gi-ye LYU-di za-ni-MA-yu-tsya **JO-ggin-gom** v ro-SSII?*

Многие люди занимаются **джоггингом** в России?

The answer, by the way, is no.

I want to work my...

ya kho-CHU ka-CHAT...

Хочу качать...

muscles.

MISH-tsi.

мышцы.

abs.
pryess.
пресс.

guns (i.e., biceps).
BAN-ki.
банки.

triceps.
TRI-tseps.
трицепс.

delts.
DYEL-tu.
дельту.

pecs.
grud-NI-ye MISH-tsi.
грудные мышцы.

thighs.
BYO-dra.
бёдра.

calves.
I-kri.
икры.

glutes.
ya-go-DI-tsi.
ягодицы.

·····Game time
po-RA i-GRAT
Пора играть

Let's play some…
po-i-GRA-yem v…
Поиграем в…

pool.
bil-YARD.
бильярд.

ping-pong.
na-STOL-nii TYE-nnis.
настольный теннис.

foosball.
KI-kyer.
кикер.

darts.
darts.
дартс.

paintball.
peint-BOL.
пейнтбол.

video games.
vi-de-o-I-gri.
видеоигры.

Let's play some Frisbee.
*da-VAI po-i-GRA-yem v **FRIZ-bi**.*
Давай поиграем в **фризби**.
Frisbee is the name of the game, but if you're referring to the actual disk, you'd use the following:

> **Let's toss around the frisbee.**
> *da-VAI po-bro-SA-yem **le-TA-yu-schu-yu ta-RYEL-ku**.*
> Давай побросаем **летающую тарелку**.
> Which is also the word for flying saucer.

Let's go bowling.
*poi-DYOM i-GRAT v **BO-u-ling**.*
Пойдем играть в **боулинг**.

I love games of chance.
*ya lyu-BLYU **a-ZART-ni-ye I-gri**.*
Я люблю **азартные игры**.

I prefer games of skill.
*ya pryed-po-chi-TA-yu **ko-MMYER-chis-ki-ye I-gri**.*
Я предпочитаю **коммерческие игры**.

If you try to cheat, I'll blow the whistle on you.
*YES-li po-pi-TA-yesh-sya **mukh-lye-VAT**, ya te-BYA vlo-ZHU.*
Если попытаешься **мухлевать**, я тебя вложу.

Let's play some cards.
da-VAI po-i-GRA-yem v KAR-ti.
Давай поиграем в карты.

Do you know how to play...?
ti u-MYE-yesh i-GRAt v...?
Ты умеешь играть в...?

poker
PO-kyer
покер

Texas hold'em
tye-KHASS-kii KHOL-dyem
Техасский холдем

Omaha poker
PO-kyer o-MA-kha
покер Омаха

Durak
du-RAK
дурак
This is without a doubt the most popular card game in Russia. The object of the game is to get rid of all your cards. The last person holding is the *durak*, or fool.

Solitaire
pa-SYANS
пасьянс

Bridge
brij
бридж

Preference
prye-fe-RANS
преферанс
This is a popular Russian variation of bridge simplified to be played without the two to six cards.

·····Chess
SHAKH-ma-ti
Шахматы

While chess may seem like a total geek "sport," it's huge in Russia and offers a powerful platform to its best competitors. Grandmaster Gary Kasparov, for instance, has organized numerous political opposition protests, even joining forces with legendary writer and all-around badass Eduard Limonov, the leader of the radical National Bolshevik Party. Now just try to tell me that only geeks play chess.

CARD SHARK)))

O-PIT-NII KAR-TYEZH-NIK

ОПЫТНЫЙ КАРТЕЖНИК

Suit	*mast*	масть
Clubs	*TRYƐ-fi*	трефы
Spades	*PI-ki*	пики
Hearts	*CHYƐR-vi*	черви
Diamonds	*BUB-ni*	бубны
Ace	*tuz*	туз
King	*ko-ROL*	король
Queen	*DA-ma*	дама
Jack	*va-LYƐT*	валет

Could you teach me to play chess?
ti bi mog me-NYA na-u-CHIT i-GRAT v SHAKH-ma-ti?
Ты бы мог меня научить играть в шахматы?

How does this piece move?
kak DVI-ga-ye-tsya E-ta fi-GU-ra?
Как двигается эта фигура?

King
ko-ROL
Король

Queen
fyerz
Ферзь
Also called королева (*ko-ro-LYE-va*).

Bishop
slon
Слон
Also called офицер (*o-fi-TSER*).

Knight
kon
Конь

Rook
la-DYA
Ладья
Also called тур (*tur*).

Pawn
PYESH-ka
Пешка

Check
shakh
Шах

Checkmate
mat
Мат

Stalemate
pat
Пат

·····Gambling
GEM-bling
Гэмблинг

But of course, the best thing about sports is the opportunity to make a little easy money off of someone else's hard work.

Illegal gambling
a-ZART-na-ya i-GRA, za-prye-SCHO-nna-ya za-KO-nom
Азартная игра, запрещённая законом

Legal gambling
a-ZART-na-ya i-GRA, raze-rye-SHO-nna-ya za-KO-nom
Азартная игра, разрешённая законом

A bet
STAV-ka
Ставка

Where's the nearest slots arcade?
*gdye SA-ma-ya bli-ZHAI-scha-ya **bo-go-DYEL-nya**?*
Где самая ближайщая **богодельня**?

He's a serious gambler.
*on sye-RYOZ-nii **i-GROK**.*
Он серьёзный **игрок**.

Do you happen to know an honest bookie?
*ti slu-CHAI-no nye ZNA-yesh CHES-no-vo **buk-MYE-ke-ra**?*
Ты случайно не знаешь честного **букмекера**?

I usually bet on the dog.
*ya o-BICH-no STAV-lyu **na dog**.*
Я обычно ставлю на **дог**.

Where can I place a bet on the game?
*gdye MOZH-no **za-KLYU-chat pa-RI** na match?*
Где можно **заключать пари** на матч?

What are the odds on the Russian National Team?
ka-KOI kyef na SBOR-nu-yu ro-SSII?
Какой кеф на Сборную России?

Oddsmaker
gan-di-KA-pper
Гандикаппер
Also called a каппер (*KA-pper*) for short.

When a bookie lengthens the odds to attract more bets
za-ma-NU-kha
Замануха

Vigorish
MAR-zha
Маржа
That is, the bookie's commission on a bet.

> **What's the over/under on this game?**
> *ka-KOI na E-tom MA-tchye niz/vyerkh?*
> Какой на этом матче низ/верх?
> Also called больше/меньше (*BOL-she/MYEN-she*).

CHAPTER 9

HUNGRY RUSSIAN

GO-LOD-NII RU-SSKII
Голодный русский

One of the great things about Russia is the food. Russians love homecookin' and are generally pretty skilled at preparing it (well, at least the women are). Precooked, prepackaged food called полуфабрикат (*po-lu-fa-bri-KAT*) is widely available, but most Russians won't eat preservative-filled crap. Which brings me to my next point. "Preservative" in Russian is консервант (*kon-ser-VANT*). The Russian cognate презерватив (*prye-zyer-va-TIV*) means condom. When enjoying a meal in Russia, try not to confuse the two.

·····Let's eat!

da-VAI po-KU-sha-yem!
Давай покушаем!

I'm hungry (masculine).
ya GO-lo-dyen.
Я голоден.

I'm hungry (feminine).
ya go-lod-NA.
Я голодна.

🍸 BORSHT MARTINI

There's no getting around it, if you're going to Russia, you're going to eat borsht. You can either garnish it with sour cream or gin. Your choice.

GET THESE:

    1 small, cooked beet
    4 sprigs thyme, divided
    ½ teaspoon prepared horseradish (optional)
    ½ ounce honey syrup*
    2 ounces London dry gin

DO THIS:

Put the beet in the bottom of a cocktail shaker with 2 of the thyme sprigs and muddle them until they're soft and squidgy. For a spicier cocktail, you can add horseradish to the beet and muddle all three together. Add the honey syrup and gin. Add ice and shake till it's well chilled. Strain into a martini glass and garnish with the other sprigs of thyme.

* For honey syrup: Add equal parts honey and water to a saucepan. Heat gently until the sugar is dissolved. Pour into a clean glass jar and store in your refrigerator for up to 1 month.

I wanna chow down.
kho-CHU po-ZHRAT.
Хочу пожрать.

You'll feel hungry as soon as you start to eat.
a-ppye-TIT pri-KHO-dit vo VRYE-mya ye-DI.
Аппетит приходит во время еды.
This is a common Russian saying.

I'm as hungry as a wolf.
ya GO-lo-dyen kak volk.
Я голоден как волк.

I'm dying of starvation.
ya u-mi-RA-yu s GO-lo-du.
Я умираю с голоду.

I can't think on an empty stomach.
ya nye mo-GU DU-mat na-to-SCHAK.
Я не могу думать **натощак**.

After work I just want to stuff my fucking face.
*PO-sle ra-BO-ti KHO-che-tsya PRO-sto **na-yeb-NUT**.*
После работы хочется просто **наебнуть**.

Do you have anything to nosh on?
*YEST u te-BYA CHTO-ni-BUD **po-KHA-vat**?*
Есть у тебя что-нибудь **похавать**?

Let's grab a bite to eat!
*da-VAI **pye-rye-KU-sim**!*
Давай **перекусим**!

Let's stop by a cafeteria.
da-VAi zai-DYOM v sto-LO-vu-yu.
Давай зайдём в столовую.
- Usually Soviet style, very cheap, and reeking of *kotlety*, mashed potatoes, cabbage, and *kompot*.

How much should we leave for a tip?
*SKOL-ko o-STA-vit **cha-ye-VIKH**?*
Сколько оставить **чаевых**?
It has become pretty common for Russian wait staff to expect a tip, no matter how lousy the service is.

Do they take plastic here?
*tut pri-ni-MA-yut **krye-DIT-ki**?*
Тут принимают **кредитки**?

Grub
ZHRACH-ka
Жрачка

Bon appétit!
pri-YAT-no-vo a-ppye-TI-ta!
Приятного аппетита!

Let's get the food on the table.
da-VAI na-KRO-yem na stol.
Давай накроем на стол.

Help yourself! Don't be shy!
u-go-SCHAI-sya! nye styes-NYAI-sya!
Угощайся! Не стесняйся!

We have more than enough!
*u nas vsye-VO **KHVA-tit s go-lo-VOI**!*
У нас всего **хватит с головой**!

VEGETARIANISM)))

VYE-GYE-TA-RI-AN-STVO
ВЕГЕТАРИАНСТВО

Vegetarianism isn't as common in the former USSR as it is in the U.S., so if you go over to someone's house for dinner, likely they will just assume you eat meat. It's generally better to warn them in advance and to be very specific about it, as some people just don't get it. Same thing goes for eating out. For example, I once went to a restaurant in Kiev and asked if a certain dish had meat in it. The waitress assured me that it did not, but when I got my order, it was covered in a sauce that was clearly full of some kind of ground beef. When I complained to the waitress, she protested that in fact the dish did not contain any meat, only the sauce did. Uh, duh. So the lesson here is that if you have dietary restrictions of any nature, don't assume anything. Spell it out for them. And double-check.

I'm a vegetarian (male).
ya vye-gye-ta-ri-AN-yets.
Я вегетарианец.

I'm a vegetarian (female).
ya vye-gye-ta-ri-AN-ka.
Я вегетарианка.

I don't eat meat or fish.
ya nye yem ni MYA-so, ni RI-bu.
Я не ем ни мясо, ни рыбу.

Is this dish **vegetarian**?
*E-to BLYU-do **vye-gye-ta-ri-AN-sko-ye**?*
Это блюдо вегетарианское?

Does this dish contain meat?
v E-tom BLYU-dye YEST MYA-so?
В этом блюде есть мясо?

I prefer **home-cooked meals**.
*ya pryed-po-chi-TA-yu **do-MASH-nyu-yu KUKH-nyu**.*
Я предпочитаю **домашнюю кухню**.

I never say no to a chance **to chow for free**.
*ya ni-kog-DA nye ot-KA-zi-va-yus ot SHAN-sa **po-KU-shat na kha-LYA-vu**.*
Я никогда не отказываюсь от шанса **покушать на халяву**.

My hotel offers a **buffet-style** breakfast.
*mo-YA gos-TI-ni-tsa pryed-la-GA-yet **SHVED-skii stol** na ZAV-trak.*
Моя гостиница предлагает **шведский стол** на завтрак.

That meat is **crazy expensive**!
*E-to MYA-so **STO-it BYE-she-ni-ye DYEN-gi**!*
Это мясо **стоит бешеные деньги**!

We've got a ton of **munchies** here.
*u nas tut **KHAV-chi-ka** na-VA-lom.*
У нас тут **хавчика** навалом.

I have a sweet tooth.
ya slad-ko-YEZH-ka.
Я сладкоежка.

I want a cheese **sandwich**.
*ya kho-CHU **bu-ter-BROD** s SI-rom.*
Я хочу **бутерброд** с сыром.

Keep in mind that *buterbrody* are generally open-faced sandwiches, so if you order a *buterbrod s sirom*, expect a slice of bread, a slab of butter, and a slice of cheese. Some places offer American-style sandwiches. These are generally called сэндвичи (*SEND-vi-chi*).

·····Fast food
fast fud
Фаст фуд

Personally, I think it's pretty lame when foreigners go to Russia and eat at McDonald's. Why on earth would you spend the time, money, and energy to travel halfway around the world just to eat the same overcooked crap that you can get at the burger joint down the street? But whatever. If you have a Mac Attack in Moscow, you will not suffer for long. McDonald's plans for world domination are nearly complete, and you can hear those familiar golden arches calling your name from just about every part of town.

Let's go to McDonald's!
poi-DYOM v Mak-DO-nalds!
Пойдём в Макдоналдс!

I'll have a...
ya BU-du...
Я буду...

> **Big Mac.**
> *big MAC.*
> Биг Мак.

> **Filet-O-Fish.**
> *fi-LE-o-FISH*
> Филе-о-фиш.

> **Cheeseburger.**
> *CHIZ-bur-ger.*
> Чизбургер.

> **Double Cheeseburger.**
> *dvoi-NOI CHIZ-bur-ger.*
> Двойной Чизбургер.

> **Chicken McNuggets.**
> *CHI-ken mak-NA-ggets.*
> Чикен Макнаггетс.

> **Quarter Pounder with Cheese.**
> *RO-yal CHIZ-bur-ger.*
> Роял Чизбургер.
> Ah yes, the Royale cheeseburger. As John Travolta astutely observes in *Pulp Fiction*: "They got the metric system there, they wouldn't know what the fuck a quarter pounder is."

> **Big N' Tasty.**
> *big TEI-sti.*
> Биг Тейсти.

That was one nasty hamburger!
*E-to bil vo-ob-SCHE **pro-TIV-nii** GAM-bur-ger!*
Это был вообще **противный** гамбургер!

Man, I love fries!
*blin, ya lyu-BLYU **fri**!*
Блин, я люблю **фри**!

Could I get some ketchup?
*MOZH-no chut **KE-tchu-pa**?*
Можно чуть **кетчупа**?

Can you get a decent pizza anywhere in Russia?

MOZH-no na-i-TI GDYE-ni-BUD v ro-SSII nor-MAL-nu-yu
PITS-tsu?

Можно найти где-нибудь в России нормальную **пиццу**?

Do you know if that pizzeria delivers?

nye ZNA-yesh, YEST li u E-toi pits-tse-RII **do-STAV-ka**
na dom?

Не знаешь, есть ли у этой пиццерии
на дом?

I think I got food poisoning from that hot dog.

po-MO-ye-mu ya o-tra-VIL-sya E-tim **khot-DO-gom**.

По-моему я отравился этим **хот-догом**.

·····I'm thirsty

mnye KHO-che-tsya pit

Мне хочется пить

I want to drink...

kho-CHU po-PIT...

Хочу попить...

Note this phrase is followed by the accusative.

some water.

vo-DICH-ku.

водичку.

Be sure to stress this word right: *vo-DICH-ku*. If you stress it
on the first syllable, it will sound like you are asking for some
vodka.

soda pop.

ga-zi-ROV-ku.

газировку.

Gazirovka is short for газированная вода (*ga-zi-RO-va-
nna-ya vo-DA*). Note that there is a Russian word сода (*SO-
da*), but that refers to baking soda.

Tarkhun.

tar-KHUN.

Тархун.

This is a kind of green-colored soda made from tarragon
and popular since Soviet times.

fruity soda.
li-mo-NAD.
лимонад.
The confusion here is that Russian *limonad* usually has little to do with what English speakers call lemonade.

birch juice.
bye-RYO-zo-vii sok.
берёзовый сок.
Who knew you could make juice from a tree?

compote.
kom-POT.
компот.
A kind of drink made from stewed fruit and sugar.

orange juice, **no ice.**
*a-pyel-SI-no-vii sok **byez I-DA**.*
апельсиновый сок **без льда**.

mineral water **on ice.**
*mi-nye-RAL-ku **so I-DOM**.*
минералку **со льдом**.

sparkling mineral water.
*mi-nye-RAL-ku **s GA-zom**.*
минералку **с газом**.

Borzhomi.
bor-ZHO-mi.
Боржоми.
A kind of salty-tasting mineral water produced in Georgia.

Narzan.
nar-ZAN.
Нарзан.
Another popular kind of mineral water.

kefir.
kye-FIR.
кефир.
Apparently, this is very good for your digestive system.

sour milk.
pro-sto-KVA-shu.
простоквашу.

kvass.
kvas.
квас.
Nonalcoholic, carbonated, usually a little bitter, and popular in summer.

·····Yum yum
nyam nyam
Ням ням

I smell something yummy.
*ya SLI-shu O-chen **VKUS-nii** ZA-pakh.*
Я слышу очень **вкусный** запах.

That's a great recipe!
*E-to KLASS-nii **rye-TSEPT**!*
Это классный **рецепт**!

What scrumptious food!
*ka-KA-ya **vku-SNYA-ti-na**!*
Какая **вкуснятина**!

Finger-lickin' good!
PAL-chi-ki ob-LI-zhesh!
Пальчики оближешь!

At the party there was a lot of yummy food.
*na vye-che-RIN-kye BI-lo MNO-go **VKUS-nyen-ko-vo**.*
На вечеринке было много **вкусненького**.

Russians love their food so, not surprisingly, they use a lot of diminutives when talking about it. While there is really no English equivalent that fully captures the meaning of most of these words, the diminutive endings convey a sense of affection, along the lines of saying "a nice, little something or other." Here are few examples of the food that Russians love to show their love to:

Pass me some nice, little bread.
*pye-rye-DAI mnye **KHLYE-bu-shek**.*
Передай мне **хлебушек**.

I adore pickled 'shrooms.
*ya o-bo-ZHA-yu za-ma-ri-NO-va-nni-ye **gri-BOCH-ki**.*
Я обожаю замаринованные **грибочки**.

I'll have wittle piece of that cakey.
*BU-du **ku-SO-chek** E-tovo **TOR-ti-ka**.*
Буду **кусочек** этого **тортика**.

These little salads are very yummy.
*E-ti **sa-LA-ti-ki** O-chen **VKUS-nyen-ki-ye**.*
Эти **салатики** очень **вкусненькие**.

I really liked that soupy.
mnye O-chen po-NRA-vil-sya E-tot SUP-chik.
Мне очень понравился этот **супчик**.

I love sweeties!
ya lyu-BLYU SLA-dyen-ko-ye!
Я люблю **сладенькое**!

Could you pass the taters?
pye-rye-DAI, po-ZHA-lui-sta, kar-TO-shech-ku.
Передай, пожалуйста, **картошечку**.

·····Yuck!
fuuuu!
Фууу!

This shit reminds me of prison swill!
Et-o gov-NO na-po-mi-NA-yet mnye o ba-LAN-dye!
Это **говно** напоминает мне о **баланде**!

That's disgusting!
E-to pro-TIV-no!
Это противно!

That looks really rank!
E-to VI-glya-dit sov-SYEM khrye-NO-vo!
Это выглядит совсем **хреново**!

That yogurt is way past its expiration date.
E-tot YO-gurt dav-NO pro-SRO-che-nii.
Этот йогурт давно **просроченный**.

This slop is inedible.
E-ta zhrat-VA nye-sye-DOB-na.
Эта **жратва** несъедобна.

I can't eat this filth!
ya nye mo-GU yest E-tu GA-dost!
Я не могу есть эту **гадость**!

This grub went bad a long time ago.
E-ta KHAV-ka dav-NO pro-PA-la.
Эта хавка давно **пропала**.

This fruit is already spoiled.
E-ti FRUK-ti u-ZHE is-POR-che-ni.
Эти фрукты уже **испорченны**.

I **burned** the chicken.
*ya **pye-rye-ZHA-ri**l KU-ri-tsu.*
Я **пережарил** курицу.

I'm afraid I **oversalted** the fish.
*bo-YUS, chto **pye-rye-so-LIL** RI-bu.*
Боюсь, что **пересолил** рыбу .

I've lost my appetite.
u me-NYA pro-PAL a-ppye-TIT.
У меня пропал аппетит.

I don't feel so well.
CHUST-vu-yu se-BYA nye O-chen.
Чувствую себя не очень.

That fish **isn't sitting right.**
*E-ta RI-ba **bi-LA nye-KSTA-ti**.*
Эта рыба **была некстати**.

I think I ate **something bad.**
*po MO-ye-mu ya cyel **CHTO-to nye TO**.*
По-моему я съел **что-то не то**.

That beef **didn't go down right.**
*E-ta go-VYA-di-na **po-PA-la nye v to GOR-lo**.*
Эта говядина **попала не в то горло**.

After trying Russian bread, I can never go back to that stale American crap.
PO-sle to-VO, kak PRO-bo-val RU-sskii khlyeb, BOL-she nye smo-GU KU-shat E-to nye-SVYE-zhe-ye ame-ri-KAN-sko-ye dyer-MO.
После того, как пробовал русский хлеб, больше не смогу кушать это несвежее американское дерьмо.

·····I'm full
ya sit
Я сыт

Refusing food in Russia is almost as hard as refusing a drink. In fact, most Russian hosts will force food on their guests with great passion and will take it as a personal insult if you don't go for seconds or thirds. Keep in mind that there is something of an unspoken rule in Russia when refusing food: The first time you refuse, no one will take you seriously. The second time, they still think you are being modest. Only after your third refusal will people start to get the hint that you've had enough.

I'm stuffed (masculine).
ya na-YEL-sya.
Я наелся.

I'm stuffed (feminine).
ya na-YE-las.
Я наелась.

I'm gonna burst!
BOL-she nye mo-GU!
Больше не могу!

I've had enough.
ya u-ZHE VSYO.
Я уже всё.

I ate too much.
ya ob-YEL-sya.
Я объелся.

I overdid it.
ya pye-rye-bor-SCHIL.
Я переборщил.

It's time for a smoke break.
*po-RA na **pye-rye-KUR**.*
Пора на **перекур**.

·····Russian food
RU-sska-ya KUKH-nya
Русская кухня

The typical Russian meal usually comprises several courses, including soup, a main course, maybe a salad or two, and plenty of bread. After Russians finish eating, they often fire up the samovar and serve tea and coffee. Here are few traditional Russian foods you might encounter:

Soups
su-PI
Супы

Borsht
Борщ
This is actually Ukrainian in origin but eaten widely in Russia as well. The main ingredient is beets, but it also usually has potatoes, carrots, cabbage, and sometimes meat. It's usually eaten со сметаной (*so smye-TA-noi*)—with sour cream.

Ukha
u-KHA
Уха
A kind of fish stew.

Schi
Щи
Cabbage soup.

Solyanka
so-LYAN-ka
Солянка
A soup of vegetables and meat, usually a little spicy.

Kharcho
khar-CHO
Харчо
A spicy Georgian soup.

Okroshka
o-KROSH-ka
Окрошка
A cold soup usually served in summer made of *kvass*, sour cream, radishes, green onion, cucumber, and sometimes potatoes and/or meat.

Salads
sa-LA-ti
Салаты

Vinegret
vi-nye-GRYET
Винегрет
A beet and vegetable salad.

Olivye
o-li-VYE
Оливье
Made of potatoes, egg, onion, mayonnaise, ham, and peas.

Meat
MYA-so
Мясо

Salo
SA-lo
Сало
Pig fat. Mmmmm! Perhaps more typical of Ukraine but eaten in Russia as well, particularly in villages.

Pelmeni
pyel-MYE-ni
Пельмени
Sort of like meat ravioli.

Cutlets
kot-LYE-ti
Котлеты

Roast
zhar-KO-ye
Жаркое

Congealed meat (or fish)
kho-lo-DYETS
Холодец

Herring salad
pod SHU-boi
Под шубой
This is like a big lump of fish salad covered with beets, eggs, potatoes, carrots, and mayonnaise.

Shashlik
shash-LIK
Шашлык
More than a food, this Caucasian version of shish kabob brings with it a whole tradition of going out to the forest, building a fire, cooking up the marinated meat, washing it down with vodka, playing guitar, and having good drunken fun.

Vareniki...
va-RYE-ni-ki...
Вареники...
These are sort of like *pelmeni* but with different kinds of fillings. In the U.S., they are usually called pierogies. The most common kinds are:

with potato
s kar-TOSH-koi
с картошкой

with cabbage
s ka-PUS-toi
с капустой

with sweet farmers cheese
s TVO-ro-gom
с творогом

with mushrooms
s gri-BA-mi
с грибами

with cherries
s VISH-nyei
с вишней

Bread
khlyeb
Хлеб

Black bread
CHOR-nii khlyeb
Чёрный хлеб

Small dried circles of bread
SUSH-ki
Сушки
Usually eaten with tea.

Gingerbread (sort of)
PRYA-ni-ki
Пряники

Pirozhki
pi-rozh-KI
Пирожки
Rolls filled with various things, most commonly potatoes, cabbage, or meat.

Dessert
dye-SYERT
Десерт

Apple pie
YA-bloch-nii pi-ROG
Яблочный пирог
This is different from American apple pie. Instead of a crust with apple filling, it is more like a cake with apple chunks baked into the batter.

Napoleon

na-po-lye-ON
Наполеон
This is a pastry with layers of flaky phyllo dough slathered with rich cream.

Bird milk

PTI-chye mo-lo-KO
Птичье молоко
This is sort of like little square pieces of marshmallow dipped in chocolate but not quite as sticky.

Bliny

bli-NI
Блины
Also sometimes called блинчики (*BLIN-chi-ki*), these are basically crepes that can be served with such things as:

> #### with honey
> *s MYO-dom*
> с мёдом
>
> #### with sweet farmers cheese
> *s TVO-ro-gom*
> с творогом
>
> #### with sour cream
> *so smye-TA-noi*
> со сметаной
>
> #### with caviar
> *s i-KROI*
> с икрой
>
> #### with jam
> *s va-RYE-nyem*
> с вареньем

Ice cream
mo-RO-zhe-no-ye
Мороженое

> **Creamy kind of ice cream**
> *plom-BIR*
> Пломбир

> **Ice cream bar**
> *es-ki-MO*
> Эскимо

·····Acknowledgments

The authors would like to thank coffee. Without you, none of our efforts would ever reach fruition. We are eternally grateful. And eternally wired.

·····About the authors

Erin Coyne holds various degrees in Russian-related fields from Fordham University, Georgetown University, and UC Berkeley, where she is currently making depressingly slow progress on a PhD in Slavic Linguistics while teaching Russian classes on the side. In a former life, she served as a Peace Corps volunteer and later worked as an NGO program director which, for better or for worse, exiled her to nearly ten long years in the former Soviet Union. Her interests include yoga, long, alcohol-fueled train rides through Eastern Europe, and TV. Lots and lots of TV. In addition to English and Russian, Erin speaks six other languages with varying degrees of success.

Igor Fisun is a native of Kiev, Ukraine, which, in moments of nationalist pride, he prefers to spell Kyiv. He is a former student of Kiev PTU where he quickly abandoned all interest in ever holding down a real job and instead embarked upon a career in freelance engraving. His native languages are Russian and Ukrainian, and he hopes someday to learn English well enough to talk his way out of a traffic ticket. His interests include cooking, Japanese art, cheap wine, and pissing people off on internet forums. He is ridiculously proud of his orchid collection.

The authors are married and live in Albany, California, with their daughter, Myroslava, and their chihuahua, Chili.